BUSINESS & ECONOMICS RESEARCH SERIES

COMPETITION AND INDUSTRY
The Irish Experience

COMPETITION AND INDUSTRY

The Irish Experience

Edited by

Dermot McAleese

Gill and Macmillan

Published in Ireland by
Gill and Macmillan Ltd
Goldenbridge
Dublin 8
with associated companies in
Auckland, Delhi, Gaborone, Hamburg, Harare,
Hong Kong, Johannesburg, Kuala Lumpur, Lagos, London,
Manzini, Melbourne, Mexico City, Nairobi,
New York, Singapore, Tokyo

Designed by
The Unlimited Design Company, Dublin
Print origination by
Design and Art Facilities, Dublin
Printed by
Billing & Sons Ltd, Worcester

British Library Cataloguing in Publication Data

Competition and industry: the Irish experience.
(Business and economics research series).
1. Ireland (Republic). Industries. Competitiveness
I. McAleese, Dermot II. Series
338.6'048'09417

ISBN 0-7171-1671-9

Contents

List of Contributors

Dermot McAleese is Whately Professor of Political Economy, Trinity College, Dublin, and editor of the Business and Economics Research Series.

Joe Durkan is Economist at Coopers and Lybrand.

Eoin O'Malley is Research Officer at the Economic and Social Research Institute.

John Bradley is Senior Research Officer at the Economic and Social Research Institute.

Charles Carroll is Senior Specialist—Marketing and Director of the PIMS programme at the Irish Management Institute.

Alan W. Gray is Managing Partner, Indecon International Economic Consultants.

Brendan M. Walsh is Professor of the National Economics of Ireland at University College, Dublin.

William Kingston is Associate Professor—(Innovation) at Trinity College, Dublin.

Leonard Wrigley is Allied Irish Bank Professor of Management at University College Cork.

INTRODUCTION

Dermot McAleese

It is appropriate that the first volume of a new series on Irish business should have competitiveness as its theme. Things went drastically wrong for the Irish economy during the past decade, because we became uncompetitive.

At a macro level the symptoms of the problem were unemployment, low growth, decline in investment, Government deficits, and heavy taxation. The macroeconomic disarray impacted on business through widespread closures, redundancies, lower profitability, crisis management, rising costs, and escalating tax bills.

The present volume addresses three major aspects of competitiveness: how it is measured, its effects on real output and employment, and how to improve it. As 1992 approaches, these issues are becoming increasingly important.

Measurement of competitiveness is a complex and difficult task. Joe Durkan outlines some of the pitfalls in standard aggregate measures such as unit labour costs, real exchange rates, and market shares. As far as cost competitiveness is concerned, he comes down, rightly in my view, in favour of using basic hourly wage rates, a measure that excludes labour productivity. By this measure, Ireland's cost position worsened significantly between 1980 and 1986. Irish hourly earnings rose by 77 per cent compared with 68 per cent in our major trading partners and 56 per cent in the UK (adjusted in each case for exchange rate changes). This job-destroying deterioration occurred simultaneously with a huge increase in unemployment and protestations of concern about lack of employment opportunities.

Durkan warns, however, against expecting any single index to tell the whole story. There is no uncomplicated answer to the question of which index best measures movements in competitiveness. Eoin O'Malley's chapter shows clearly why: firms have divergent cost structures. Take, for example, the proportion of total costs accounted for by wages and salaries. It varies from 25 per cent in clothing, footwear and leather to 8 per cent in food processing. Probing deeper, O'Malley's statistics show that indigenous clothing firms in turn are much more labour-intensive (wages and salaries 36 per cent of costs) than Irish subsidiaries of overseas clothing firms. Similarly, in the case of telephone, fuel and energy costs, the impact differs depending on the type of firm involved—obvious in a way, but the chapter breaks new ground in quantifying by how much cost structures differ among industries and nationality of firm.

It is worth emphasising that individual cost categories ultimately should be related to value added, or better still profits, not total costs, in an analysis of competitiveness. This lesson has been fully absorbed in the literature on protection, where effective tariffs have replaced nominal tariffs as a measure of the protective effect of import barriers. Interest costs amount to 2 per cent of total manufacturing costs but to 25 per cent of profits (and an even higher proportion of distributed profits). On this arithmetic, a 50 per cent rise in interest rates would result in an increase of only one percentage point in total costs—but would cut profits by 12 per cent. Again, a comment about the use of averages is in order: the effect on a firm's profitability is evidently going to depend on its individual cost structure.

Devising a competitiveness index may be a complex exercise but it is child's play by comparison with the problems of measuring the effects of changes in competitiveness. John Bradley brings the sophistication of the ESRI's medium-term model (of which he is the major architect) to bear on this subject. He identifies profitability as the key indicator of competitiveness, which is no more than the obverse side of costs, and finds evidence to confirm the importance of competitiveness. A loss of 1 per cent in competitiveness results in a 0.4 per cent loss in Ireland's share of world capacity output. He shows that, in a small open economy, competitiveness works in two ways: affecting domestic firms' willingness to expand capacity in Ireland and foreign firms' willingness to locate new activities in Ireland. The identification and attempted measurement of these effects is a novel and important contribution to our understanding of the subject.

Charles Carroll approaches the same problem from a different but complementary perspective. His perspective is that of corporate planner or market strategist rather than economist. No matter how tightly costs are controlled, at macro and micro level, firms will not flourish without careful attention to their positioning in the market. Market share is here the main focus of attention. He warns that 'a 1 per cent share of any market, however big, will not yield an adequate return,' and he questions the efficiency of a consumer brands approach for a country at Ireland's level of development. Instead the case is made for concentrating on carefully segmented industrial buyers' markets. The empirical basis for his work is the massive PIMS data file, which has been explained in detail in his book on the subject.

So, competitiveness can be measured, and it does matter. But how do we improve it?

This has been the subject of numerous reports, white papers and speeches over the years, going back to the prodigious output of the NESC under the chairmanship of Professor Louden Ryan, continued in the Baker, McAleese and Walsh *Report of the Committee on Costs and Competitiveness,* commissioned by the Minister for Finance in 1981 and powerfully invoked again in the NESC's 1986 report, *Strategy for Economic Growth.* The various strands in the debate are summarised with enviable precision by Alan Gray. He writes with authority, having once served as chairman of the industrial costs monitoring body, an inter-departmental group set up by the Coalition Government in response to concern about these matters. On labour costs, he recommends pay policy for the public sector only, letting the market exercise discipline over pay rises in the private sector. He stresses the need for attention to the scandalously high absenteeism rate in Ireland. The tax wedge is seen as a serious barrier to competitiveness. He stresses the role of the Government in setting a tax and interest rate environment more conducive to low costs. A powerful theme in his argument is the desirability of using competition or deregulation rather than direct controls as a means of curbing costs in both public and private sectors.

Competitiveness is a relative thing. In a trade-oriented country, the important point is to be competitive relative to overseas competitors. Since Ireland obviously cannot exercise control over foreign costs, there are two variables left—domestic costs (which have been discussed by Gray) and the exchange rate—with which to influence the domestic/overseas cost ratio. Brendan Walsh analyses the relevance of exchange rate policy to competitiveness. That there is any relationship between the two is itself a matter of debate, but Walsh comes down firmly for the view that Irish exchange rate policy should be concerned with maintaining competitiveness as well as with curbing inflation. With regard to the EMS, he concludes that Ireland has enjoyed some benefits from membership but that a price has been paid in the form of deteriorating competitiveness. The OECD-based chart in his chapter, showing the relative wage position of Ireland in 1978–87 (fig. 7.1), deserves careful study. It estimates the size of the competitiveness loss as 20 per cent since 1978. One gain from the EMS, not apparent when Walsh's chapter was being written, was lower interest rates. The combination of strong Irish fiscal policy and a jittery market in sterling kept our rates low relative to UK rates, with a gap of four percentage points opening up in autumn 1988.

Much has been written about the importance of innovation and of research and development (R&D) in determining a country's competitiveness. William Kingston offers a novel analysis of what might be done to improve the profitability and effectiveness of innovation in Ireland. Criticising Irish credulity about the usefulness of direct Government action, he argues that providing more legal protection to innovation (along lines that have been detailed in his book) would be much more cost-efficient than spending money directly on R&D. His other proposal is to increase revenue from patent fees and to use the proceeds as a venture seed-capital fund for small innovating enterprises. His recommendations carry a unique advantage in being operational at virtually zero cost to the exchequer.

Leonard Wrigley brings matters to a close with a wide-ranging review of where Ireland stands in the competitiveness league and how its position can be improved. He draws on the European Management Forum Report, which regularly documents some thirty-five indicators of each country's competitive position (truly it *is* a complex concept). Wrigley is a strong critic of Irish economic policy—a policy he considers as militating against economic responsibility, encouraging passivity, and altogether inappropriate for a small trading country that has to live on its wits in a highly competitive world. 'The logic of an elephant is power: of a flea it is hustle.' This memorable phrase summarises the message of a sophisticated analysis. Applied to Ireland, small, says Wrigley, means hustle (a clever variation on the 'small is beautiful' theme!). In plainer language, Wrigley wants to see Irish business develop speed in creating product quality, marketing effectiveness, and direct labour productivity. Through a series of MBA theses at UCC he has played a pioneering role in forging closer links between economics and business disciplines in an effort to deepen our understanding of business strategy in a peripheral economy.

This introductory narrative can do no more than give a flavour of the line of argument and the headline conclusions of the contributors. The topic is clearly interesting and important, and the contributors—all experts in their own fields—have developed their analysis with authority. Let the editor stand no longer between them and the reader.

HOW TO MEASURE COMPETITIVENESS

Joe Durkan

Coopers and Lybrand

Competitiveness is a characteristic of firms and economies.

A firm is competitive if, at prevailing prices for its products and inputs, it can generate sufficient profits to maintain its existence.

An economy is essentially different. An economy could have all firms competitive in the sense used above, but simultaneously have unemployed resources, given the cost structure that prevails. A competitive economy is one where resources are fully utilised and admits of the possibility that some firms are decaying and others expanding.

While the concept of competitiveness is straightforward both at the firm and economy level, tests of competitiveness are less clear-cut. Because of a lack of detailed company information, tests of competitiveness appropriate to the firm have tended to be applied to highly aggregated data, and conclusions have been drawn about the degree of national or economy-wide competitiveness. Strictly one should look at firms, and then apply different criteria to the national economy.

At the level of the firm an assessment of competitiveness involves a discussion of its profitability and the factors that influence profitability. These include products and prices; market share and marketing; operating costs (including labour costs); capital stock; and management. A competitive firm tends to embody unique characteristics and strengths, which differentiate it from its competitors. These competitors may also exhibit unique characteristics. While in a pedagogic sense we abstract differences between firms, the reality in the market is that firms and their products have real or perceived strengths and weaknesses.

It is apparent from this view of the competitiveness of a firm that many factors that influence a firm's competitive position are unquantifiable or qualitative in nature. As a consequence, and particularly when one goes from the firm to the economy in the loose sense referred to earlier, measures of competitiveness are really measures of those things that are easy to get figures for. In effect, when one is looking at national competitiveness using the firm as a basis, this involves a discussion of prices, costs and market share in an aggregate sense, where these factors are compared with those of other countries. Furthermore, as we rarely have absolute data it is trends over time that are generally considered.

PRICES

At an aggregate level, trends in price competitiveness have to be approached indirectly. There are no price indices for tradable goods and services. Instead it is possible to compare unit values for actually traded goods, or wholesale prices for all goods. Both suffer serious drawbacks, so much so that a comparison of price competitiveness based on both can be misleading. Unit values are not prices. Unit values of exports could be increasing relative to unit values in other countries simply because of an improvement in the quality of products relative to other countries or because of changes in the product mix.

Wholesale prices include the prices of goods that are not traded internationally, and of course include the prices of foodstuffs—much of which are influenced by the CAP, often operating differently between countries (Ireland and the UK being the notable example).

These difficulties should not be underestimated. It is widely believed that if trends in 'true' prices for tradables were available they would indicate no difference between trends in Ireland and elsewhere, because Ireland is simply a price taker.

Over and above these issues, volatility in exchange rates creates unique difficulties for the interpretation of the data. Prices, however measured, have to be compared across countries in common currency terms. A significant portion of a loss or gain in measured price competitiveness in the short term tends to be due to exchange rate changes—yet most firms exporting would be unaffected by this, because of hedging operations in the foreign exchange market. Of course volatility is not the only characteristic of exchange rates. There are also medium-term trends, for example the strength of the dollar up to early 1985 and its weakness since. These trends can be very disruptive. The critical factor for firms is the extent to which gains that are solely due to exchange rate changes are embodied in behaviour, for example in wage rates and investment. To the extent that firms regard an exchange rate change as permanent and behave accordingly, medium-term trends will necessitate major rationalisation once the direction of the exchange rate changes. Where prices are externally determined, of course, measures of price competitiveness will show no change, irrespective of what is happening to profits.

COSTS

As a result of the difficulties of defining precise price variables to examine price competitiveness, and the difficulty with the concept itself in the context of a price-taking model for a country such as Ireland, attention is generally directed to costs.

Unfortunately, we have no information on total production costs on a reasonably current basis. Information is, however, available on wage costs and on the costs of public utilities. Discussion of costs then tends to be a discussion of changes in wage rates, changes in wages per unit of output, and absolute levels of public utility charges, with greatest attention devoted to wages.

In general the focus has been on trends in unit wage costs, i.e. wage costs per unit of output. The logic behind a consideration of unit wage costs is that a rise in measured unit wage costs relative to other countries (in common currency terms) represents a fall in competitiveness.

It is not obvious that this is necessarily the case. First, it is necessary to establish the link between wage costs and total costs, and between total costs and competitiveness. Second, measures of unit wage costs, particularly in Ireland, can be heavily influenced by structural change, start-up firms and sectors being high-wage, while decaying sectors and firms tend to be low-wage. Third, unit wage cost is not a variable in its own right. Unit wage cost is derived by looking at total wages divided by total output, and is equivalent to wages per person divided by output per person. Output is not independent of wage rates, nor are wage rates independent of output. Fourth, the form in which new wage agreements are set can influence unit wage costs. If agreements are front-loaded, unit wage costs tend to increase first and then decline. Fifth, unit wage costs can vary depending on the business cycle. If demand weakens and output falls, measured unit wage costs increase, and vice versa. Sixth, wage costs are not the same as labour costs. For these reasons unit wage cost as a variable by itself must be treated with caution.

Changes in basic rates of pay are often considered a better indicator of changes in cost competitiveness. This gets over some of the difficulties with unit wage costs referred to above, but suffers in turn from the fact that a significant increase in basic rates of pay that simply matched a significant increase in productivity could be seen as a worsening in competitiveness.

Finally on the wages front, in some respects what is important to firms is the absolute level of labour costs relative to competitors. If firms and economies were in equilibrium, differences in wages would reflect different factor endowments of one sort or another. However, the reality is that the world is characterised by no such equilibrium. If wage rates here are significantly higher than, say, in the UK, there is an incentive for firms to relocate just on wage cost grounds, irrespective of recent trends in unit wage costs or trends in wage rates.

In addition to data on wage costs, however defined, some information is available on public utility costs (electricity, gas, communications, transport) in Ireland relative to other countries. These show in general a deterioration in costs to consumers since the mid-1970s relative to other countries.[1]

The principal difficulty with measures of cost competitiveness is that by concentrating on readily available data they ignore the total cost structure of firms. At a more fundamental level we need to know why differences have emerged in costs and how these have impacted on the overall cost structure. If wage rates have risen too rapidly relative to other countries, what has been the pressure point on the demand side and on the supply side? Why have firms been willing to make payments? Have wage increases been heavily influenced by the taxation policy of the Government, and have other non-wage costs been influenced by Government action? How have firms reacted to a reduction in competitiveness: by going under or rationalising?

MARKET SHARE

An alternative approach to evaluating competitiveness is to look at trade performance. The logic behind this is that if a country is increasing its share of world trade, this is evidence that the economy is competitive. This is not necessarily the case. As is well known, Ireland's share of world trade has increased sharply over the past fifteen years. The prime source of this growth was the establishment in Ireland of branches of multinationals producing goods for export, where the main competitive element derived from the tax treatment of profits through export sales relief. It is not a necessary condition for growth in market share that firms be price or cost-competitive once tax-based activities are considered.

Even if tax-based exports are excluded, a country could find that shifts in demand patterns, with no change in costs or prices, could result in an increase in market share, because firms had been established in the right market areas. In effect this would represent an increase in competitiveness.

PRICE COMPETITIVENESS,
COST COMPETITIVENESS AND MARKET SHARE: CONCLUSION

The traditional approaches to the measurement of competitiveness are seriously flawed. To some extent this comes from attempting to apply at the national level concepts that are partial explanations of the performance of companies. At a national level there are no adequate measures of price that would enable one to see if prices domestically of traded goods were moving adversely (never mind the question of the level of those prices). Given a model of price determination that sees tradable goods prices as externally determined, emerging price differences could be seen as evidence of faulty data. Existing measures of cost competitiveness are also defective. They concentrate on a narrow range of costs (labour and utilities) and ignore the total cost structure. Market share analysis is affected by tax-based production and trading.

Having said all this, it is still useful to look at aggregates—but not to expect any one to provide a single, uncomplicated answer to the question of competitiveness.[2] Trends in wage rates, hourly earnings, exchange-rate-adjusted prices and market shares all provide signals. It is a question of reconciling conflicting signals. In many respects these signals are simply the starting-point for further analysis.

AN ALTERNATIVE APPROACH TO COMPETITIVENESS

It was stated earlier that part of the difficulty with measures of competitiveness is that they represent an attempt to apply at a national level what are really measures appropriate to the individual firm. An alternative approach is to look at the competitive position of firms separately, building that up into a picture of individual sectors, while applying different tests for the economy as a whole.

It is firms that trade, so the natural starting-point is the firm level. The questions relevant to an assessment of the competitiveness of a firm relate to its profitability, and this will be determined by its product mix; the prices of its products; its marketing; the capital stock; the utilisation of that stock; the number and quality of its labour force; wage rates and non-wage labour costs; inputs, their availability and prices; transport, communications and other utility prices; management; and so on. The development of profitability over time can be considered, distinguishing between those factors that are internal to the firm and those that are external. The sector is an amalgam of individual firms. Over time the development of the sector can be explained by reference to competitive factors within the sector and by external influences. This type of analysis would throw up the impact of public policy (such as taxation, exchange rates, public utility pricing) on firms, as well as long-run trends (such as competition from newly industrialising countries).

At the national level the real test of competitiveness is the extent to which the economy maintains internal and external balance in the medium term. Is the economy growing at a reasonable level, given the growth in the labour force and the capital stock? Can the quality of both be improved? Are markets functioning to the extent that, at current wage rates, labour is fully employed? Is there fiscal balance? Is the balance of payments in equilibrium?

The national level adds an extra dimension to firm and sector analysis. It is quite possible for firms and sectors to be in some form of equilibrium and competitive but for the economy to be experiencing unemployment because of labour market rigidities or tax rates that caused a shake-out of labour.

Finally, it is as well to recognise that even in those cases where firms are competitive and the economy is uncompetitive in the sense used here, there may be very little that can be done. The present situation and how it is likely to evolve over the future is a case in point.

The economy is currently adjusting to a restoration of fiscal balance. As a consequence of the reduction in demand associated with this adjustment, the balance of payments is now in surplus, and as the adjustment proceeds a surplus seems likely to remain. The corporate sector, in general, has adjusted its scale of operations to reflect the new lower level of demand, and those firms that remain in business have restored profitability. Unemployment, however, is very high. The scale of unemployment is greater than might have been expected given the fall in demand that occurred, as firms were also forced to rationalise on foot of a deterioration in the wage/price ratio—a consequence of the tax increases of the early 1980s. Effectively, if firms are in equilibrium and if there is high unemployment in an open economy, that economy is cost-constrained. There is no policy instrument available to the Government to break out of this impasse. To the extent that anything can be done it is in the area of labour market policies, but the effects of these are medium to long-term.

Notes

1. P. Fisher, 'The Cost Environment of Irish Industry' (paper read to the Industrial Studies Association), 1987.
2. T. Baker, D. McAleese, and B.M. Walsh, *Report of the Committee on Costs and Competitiveness*, Dublin: Stationery Office (Pl. 154) 1981.

COST STRUCTURES IN IRISH INDUSTRY

Eoin O'Malley

Economic and Social Research Institute

Costs can have a significant influence on the competitiveness of industry, although they are not the only determinants of competitive success. 'Non-price' factors, such as product quality, efficiency in production, marketing and reliability of delivery can be very important too. In assessing the effect on competitiveness of different types of costs, it is necessary not only to examine how Irish costs compare with those in other countries but also to consider how significant each cost item is in industry's overall cost structure. This chapter concentrates on presenting data on cost structures in Irish industry, and it includes some discussion of the implications for competitiveness.

TABLE 3.1 **Cost Structure of Irish Manufacturing Industry**

CENSUS OF INDUSTRIAL PRODUCTION	COSTS AS PERCENTAGE OF GROSS OUTPUT, 1984	COSTS AS PERCENTAGE OF SALES, 1983		IDA SURVEY
Materials and 'industrial' services	58.1		52.8	Materials
Fuel & power	3.1		3.4	Fuel & energy
Wages & salaries	12.9		17.7	Labour costs
			13.2	Purchased services
			1.9	Interest
Remainder of net output	25.9	26.2	3.0	Depreciation, leasing
			0.1	Rent
			8.0	Profit
	100	100		

Sources: CSO, *Census of Industrial Production, 1984* for column 1; revised data from IDA survey[1] for column 2.

Table 3.1 shows the principal cost items as a percentage of gross output or sales of manufacturing as a whole (with data taken from two different sources, which use somewhat different classifications).

It can be seen that material inputs are of major importance, accounting for more than half of total costs. About 40 per cent of the materials used by industry are imported, while the remaining 60 per cent is supplied by domestic sources. It should be noted that the cost of production of the domestically supplied materials includes some expenditure in the Irish economy on non-materials items such as wages and purchased services. Thus the total influence of Irish non-materials costs, both directly and indirectly, through their influence on materials costs, is somewhat greater than it appears from table 3.1.

Nevertheless, materials remain much the largest cost to industry. Industrial firms may have little control over materials prices, although astute purchasing can make a difference. Probably more importantly, companies can influence their materials costs by the efficiency of their production process, materials management, and product design, which determine how efficiently materials are used and how much is wasted.

After materials inputs, the next most important costs are purchased services and wages and salaries, at about 13 per cent of total costs each, with other labour costs (apart from wages and salaries) accounting for a further 3 to 5 per cent of total costs.[2] Almost 30 per cent of the service inputs are purchased abroad, principally by Irish subsidiaries of foreign multinational companies. Many of these imported services are provided on an intra-firm basis by overseas affiliate companies, at prices that are little influenced by Irish domestic factors. The cost of the domestically supplied services, however, would be influenced by Irish labour costs and other local factors.

Industry purchases a wide range of services, such as transport, maintenance and repair, advertising, insurance, financial and professional services, postal and telecommunications services, cleaning, catering, and security. There is evidence that a number of these costs—including transport, insurance, post and telecommunications—are relatively high in Ireland,[3] but little precise information is available on the significance of most of these individual items in industry's overall cost structure. In the case of post and telecommunications, data published by the Department of Industry and Commerce indicate that these two services combined accounted for 0.9 to 1.2 per cent of total costs of native Irish-owned industries in 1984. And it may be roughly estimated that the cost of employers' liability and commercial property insurance in 1986 amounted to about 0.5 per cent of costs in manufacturing, with a likely maximum estimate of 0.9 per cent.[4]

As shown in table 3.1, the remaining costs not already mentioned are spread over a number of relatively small items, which each account for up to about 3 per cent of the total. Fuel and power, which accounted for 3.1 per cent of manufacturing gross output in 1984, may be broken down into 1.4 per cent for petroleum oils, 1.3 per cent for electricity, and 0.4 per cent for other energy sources. After all costs were accounted for, 8 per cent of the value of sales was left as profits for manufacturing as a whole.

It is clear from the figures that some costs are far more important for competitiveness than others. Thus, for example, going by the figures in column 2 of table 3.1, if materials costs were 2 per cent higher for Irish firms than for competitors abroad, this would have an impact on total direct costs equivalent to a 6 per cent excess cost for labour, a 31 per cent higher charge for fuel and energy, or a 56 per cent cost penalty for interest.

INDIGENOUS AND FOREIGN INDUSTRY

The simple aggregate figures for all manufacturing in table 3.1, however, conceal a great deal of diversity between different categories of industry. One important distinction is that between Irish indigenous and foreign-owned industries, which have rather different cost structures. Table 3.2 shows that industrial inputs (meaning materials, industrial services, fuel and power) account for a considerably larger proportion of the gross output of indigenous industry, at 70.5 per cent, than of foreign-owned industry, at 52 per cent. Wages and salaries also account for a somewhat higher proportion of the costs of indigenous firms than of foreign firms, despite the fact that average wages are lower in the indigenous sector, as is seen in the bottom half of table 3.2.

TABLE 3.2 **Cost Structure of Indigenous and Foreign-Owned Manufacturing Industry (Costs as Percentage of Gross Output, 1984)**

	INDIGENOUS	FOREIGN-OWNED
Industrial inputs	70.5	52.0
Wages & salaries	14.7	11.0
Remainder of net output	14.9	37.0
Wages & salaries per person engaged (£)	8,500	9,700
Net output per person engaged (£)	17,100	42,500

Note: Industrial inputs are materials, 'industrial' services, fuel and power.
Source: CSO, *Census of Industrial Production, 1984.*

In general, therefore, foreign firms are in higher value-added activities, i.e. their value added to industrial inputs accounts for a greater proportion of their gross output. And they also have much higher labour productivity than indigenous firms, since their net output per employee is far higher, as seen in the bottom row of table 3.2. Relatively high levels of value-added or labour productivity can result from factors such as a relatively high degree of capital-intensity, strong technological capabilities, strong marketing capabilities, highly developed specialised skills, or relatively efficient management. In the high-value-added, high-productivity activities in which such factors are of greatest importance, input costs would generally be less important for competitive success than in other industries, since competitiveness depends less on costs and prices and more on factors such as product quality, innovation, marketing, and quality of skills.

There are also costs associated with these factors, such as expenditure on research and development, training, advertising, and the establishment and maintenance of distribution networks. But in the case of most foreign-owned firms in Ireland, much of these costs are borne outside the country by other branches of the same company, so that they are not part of the Irish operation's cost structure. Hence the cost environment in Ireland would not be of major importance for these aspects of foreign companies' competitiveness.

SECTORAL DIFFERENCES IN COST STRUCTURES

Apart from the distinction between indigenous and foreign-owned industries, there are also substantial differences between the cost

TABLE 3.3 **Cost Structures as Percentage of Gross Output, by Manufacturing Sector, 1984**

SECTOR	INDUSTRIAL INPUTS	WAGES & SALARIES	REMAINDER OF NET OUTPUT	AVERAGE WAGE (£000)	NET OUTPUT PER EMPLOYEE (£000)	WAGES AS PERCENTAGE OF NET OUTPUT
Non-metallic mineral products	53.1	19.0	27.9	10.5	25.7	40.5
Chemicals	44.0	8.9	47.2	12.2	77.2	15.8
Metals & engineering	54.9	13.6	31.5	9.0	29.8	30.2
Food	77.0	8.3	14.7	8.8	24.4	36.0
Drink & tobacco	42.9	18.6	38.5	13.1	40.0	32.6
Textiles	65.0	18.9	16.1	7.4	13.9	53.9
Clothing, footwear & leather	58.3	24.7	17.0	5.4	9.0	59.3
Timber & wooden furniture	59.4	22.3	18.2	6.1	10.7	55.1
Paper & paper products, printing & publishing	44.9	29.2	25.9	10.2	19.1	53.0
Miscellaneous industries	71.0	12.2	16.8	8.5	20.2	42.1
Total	61.2	12.9	25.9	9.0	26.9	33.2

Source: CSO, *Census of Industrial Production, 1984.*

structures of different manufacturing sectors. Table 3.3 shows the basic data for the ten broad classes of manufacturing. It can be seen from column 1 of the table that industrial inputs account for less than 45 per cent of gross output in the relatively high value-added sectors of chemicals, drink and tobacco, and paper products and printing. In contrast, they account for as much as 77 per cent of gross output in the low value-added food sector, which is largely engaged in basic processing of local primary products. There is also great variation in the figures for wage costs as a percentage of gross output, ranging from 8 per cent in food to 29 per cent in paper products and printing.

There are a number of different reasons for these variations in the importance of wage costs in industrial cost structures. In the food sector, for example, wage *rates* are about the same as the average for manufacturing as a whole, at £8,800 per annum in 1984, and wages account for a similar proportion of net output (or value added to industrial inputs) as in total manufacturing. But wages are a small proportion of total costs, because value added (or net output) is relatively low in relation to gross output. In the chemicals sector, on the other hand, wages account for a similarly low proportion of total costs as a result of a quite different combination of factors. The chemicals industry has high wage rates, but this is accompanied by extremely high value added to industrial inputs, so that wages account for a very low proportion of net output and hence also a relatively low proportion of gross output. Or, to take an industry with a very different cost structure, clothing, footwear and leather has exceptionally low wage rates, and about average value added to material inputs. But it also has a particularly labour-intensive production process, as reflected in the high proportion of wage costs in net output. The result is that wage costs account for about double the average proportion of gross output, despite the low wage rates.

This variety of factors influencing the proportionate importance of wage costs in total costs means that wage costs as a percentage of gross output is not necessarily a reliable indicator of the importance of wage cost competitiveness for an industry's overall competitive success. For example, if we compare drink and tobacco with textiles, wage costs account for the same proportion of gross output in these two sectors. But drink and tobacco has much higher average wage rates, higher value added to industrial inputs, and higher net output per employee. In other words, compared with textiles, the drink and tobacco industry is a high-value-added, high-productivity industry, as a result of factors such as high capital-intensity, substantial economies of scale, and strong marketing, accompanied by product differentiation. For these reasons, the drink and tobacco industry can pay considerably higher wages than textiles without being forced out of business; thus it seems that the overall competitiveness of drink and tobacco does not depend so much on low wages, despite the fact that wage costs account for the same proportion of its total costs as in textiles.

As a rule of thumb, industries that can pay relatively high wages and have high net output per employee—such as drink and tobacco, or chemicals—would generally be least sensitive to considerations of labour cost competitiveness, since they are defensible against competitors on other grounds (which enables them to pay high wages in the first place). At the other extreme are the industries that pay low wages and have low net output per employee, with wages accounting for a high proportion of that net output. These industries—such as textiles, clothing, footwear and leather, and timber and wooden furniture—are likely to be most sensitive to considerations of labour cost competitiveness.

TYPES OF COST STRUCTURES

It was shown in table 3.3 that there is considerable variation between the cost structures of different industries when manufacturing is divided into ten broad classes. Even greater variability is found when industries are subdivided still further. Data from the Census of Industrial Production or the IDA survey allow one to distinguish between thirty to forty different sectors, which can be further divided into indigenous and foreign-owned components.

A very wide range of cost structures is found among the resulting industrial categories; but such diversity is bewildering unless some effort is made to classify the industries according to types of cost structures.

TABLE 3.4 **Cost Structures of Selected Industries as a Percentage of Sales, 1983**

	TOTAL MANUFACTURING	INDIGENOUS MEAT PROCESSING	FOREIGN OFFICE AND DATA PROCESSING MACHINERY	INDIGENOUS CLOTHING
Materials	52.8	82.2	47.3	49.6
Fuel & energy	3.4	1.5	0.6	1.7
Industrial inputs	56.2	83.7	47.9	51.3
Labour costs	17.7	8.3	8.2	35.8
Purchased services	13.2	4.9	18.4	11.8
Interest, depreciation, rent	4.9	1.7	3.1	3.5
Profit	8.0	1.5	22.4	−2.3
Total value added	43.8	16.3	52.1	48.7
Total	100	100	100	100
Average labour cost (£)	9,960	8,820	10,653	5,730
Value added per employee (£)	24,630	17,370	67,770	7,800
Labour cost as percentage of value added	40.4	50.8	15.7	73.5

Note: Totals may not add correctly due to rounding. Source: Revised data from IDA survey.

As a step towards such a classification, table 3.4 shows the cost structures of a selection of disaggregated industries that have distinctive characteristics representing certain types. Column 1 shows the average cost structure of total manufacturing for purposes of comparison. By comparison with this average, material inputs account for a very high percentage of the value of sales in indigenous meat processing, so that all other costs in that sector are substantially below the average percentage. This is a low-value-added or basic processing industry. The growth or decline of such an industry depends substantially on the availability of material inputs for processing, and the cost of those inputs.

The main distinctive feature of the foreign-owned office and data processing machinery sector is high labour productivity (or high value added per employee). As a result of this feature, labour costs account for a low percentage both of total costs and value added, despite higher than average wage rates. This sector also combines relatively high wages with high profits, as a result of high labour productivity.

Finally, the main distinctive feature of the indigenous clothing sector is low labour productivity (or low value added per employee). As a result of this feature, labour costs account for a particularly high percentage both of total costs and value added, despite the fact that wage rates are well below the average. This sector combines low wages with poor profitability as a result of low productivity.

Many industrial sectors have cost structures that are broadly comparable to one or other of the examples in table 3.4. Because of limitations of space it is not possible to present all the relevant data here, but the classifications that follow are based on examination of cost data both from the Census of Industrial Production and the IDA survey.

BASIC PROCESSING INDUSTRIES

The basic processing industries, in which industrial inputs account for at least 80 per cent of total costs, are:

(a) Both the indigenous and foreign-owned branches of dairy products, meat processing, grain milling and animal feed, and leather;

(b) The indigenous (but not the foreign-owned) branch of 'other' industries (including oil refining).

In these industries the material inputs are mostly primary products produced in Ireland, and the supply and quality of inputs is probably a very significant determinant of the performance of the processing industries. The indigenous 'other' industries sector is an exception here, since it is primarily engaged in oil refining—using imported inputs. These basic processing industries accounted for 13 per cent of manufacturing employment and 10 per cent of manufacturing net output in 1984.

HIGH-PRODUCTIVITY INDUSTRIES

If we define the high-productivity industries as those in which net output or value added per employee is ranked among the top one-third of all industries, the sectors in this group are:

(a) Both the indigenous and foreign-owned branches of basic industrial chemicals, office and data processing machinery, and drink and tobacco;
(b) The foreign-owned (but not the indigenous) branches of non-metallic mineral products, pharmaceuticals, remainder of chemicals, metals, mechanical engineering, electrical engineering, instrument engineering, 'other' food, paper and paper products, and plastic processing.

Thus, most of the high-productivity industries are foreign-owned, although a few indigenous industries are included. Wage rates in a majority of the industries included here are relatively high (i.e. among the top one-third of industries), and they are in the medium range in the remainder. Despite the relatively high wage rates, wages as a percentage of gross output are in the low or medium range in all cases, and wages as a percentage of net output are in the low range (i.e. in the lowest one-third of industries) in all cases. In addition, profits as a percentage of sales are in the high range in nearly all cases.

Thus in this group of industries, relatively high wages are generally combined with high profits and a low influence of labour costs in the overall cost structure. These are the industries that are probably least sensitive to the cost environment, particularly the cost of labour, owing to high value added and high productivity, giving them a relatively defensible position. The foreign-owned high-productivity industries also import a relatively high proportion of their inputs, which isolates them further from the influence of the Irish cost environment. The high-productivity industries listed above accounted for 29 per cent of manufacturing employment and 57 per cent of manufacturing net output in 1984.

LOW-PRODUCTIVITY INDUSTRIES

The industries with the lowest labour productivity are those listed below. In these sectors, net output per employee is ranked among the lowest one-third of all industries:
(a) Both the indigenous and foreign-owned branches of bread and flour confectionery, knitting, footwear, clothing, and timber and wooden furniture;
(b) The indigenous branches only of pharmaceuticals, metal articles, mechanical engineering, electrical engineering, motor vehicles, other means of transport, instrument engineering, 'other' food, wool, 'other' textiles.

Most of these are indigenous industries, although the foreign-owned branches of the sectors with the lowest labour productivity are included too. Wage rates in a large majority of the industries included here are low (i.e. among the lowest one-third of industries), and they are at the low end of the medium range in all of the rest except one. But despite the generally low wages, wage costs are high as a percentage of net output in all cases and as a percentage of gross output in most cases. Profits are low too in most of these industries, at a few per cent of sales or less, although there are exceptions with good profits, including two of the foreign industries included here.

In most of this group of industries, therefore, low wages are combined with low profits and a high influence of labour costs in the cost structure. This group probably includes the industries that are most sensitive to cost considerations, especially labour costs. As a notable exception to these generalisations, indigenous 'other' means of transport pays high wages and is quite profitable; its labour productivity is relatively low because it is largely engaged in highly labour-intensive repair and maintenance of aircraft and railway equipment, rather than production. Significant parts of a few of the other industries, especially bread and flour confectionery and the indigenous branches of metal articles, mechanical engineering and electrical engineering, are engaged in highly local market-oriented activities; these activities are sheltered to some degree from foreign competition, although there may be quite intense competition between domestic firms. The low-productivity industries above accounted for 34 per cent of manufacturing employment and 15 per cent of manufacturing net output in 1984.

OTHER INDUSTRIES

The remaining industries, which fit into none of the groups already mentioned, are:

(a) Both the indigenous and foreign-owned branches of sugar and sugar confectionery, printing and publishing, and rubber products;
(b) The indigenous branches only of non-metallic mineral products, remainder of chemicals, metals, paper and paper products, and plastic processing;
(c) The foreign-owned branches only of metal articles, motor vehicles, 'other' means of transport, wool, 'other' textiles, and 'other' industries.

In these industries, net output per employee is in the medium range, and value added to material inputs is above the basic processing level. These industries combined accounted for 24 per cent of manufacturing employment and 18 per cent of manufacturing net output in 1984. The principal cost features of most of the sectors included here generally fall within the medium range among all industries. In other words, value added to material inputs, wage rates, and wages as a percentage of net or gross output, are mostly in the medium range, while profit rates tend to be low to medium with the foreign-owned industries generally being somewhat more profitable than the indigenous ones. A few exceptional cases are indigenous printing and publishing and non-metallic mineral products, and foreign-owned motor vehicles, which have relatively high wage rates with wages being a rather high proportion of total costs. This may be due to the fact that these industries had a degree of natural or artificial protection against foreign competition.

ENERGY AND INTEREST COSTS

Finally, energy and interest costs are of limited importance for most sectors and for manufacturing as a whole, but they have a more significant impact on certain industries. Fuel and power accounted for 3.1 per cent of total manufacturing costs in 1984, and less in a large majority of industries. But this item accounted for over 10 per cent of costs in basic industrial chemicals (including fertilisers) and man-made fibres, and between 5 and 10 per cent in metals, non-metallic mineral products, rubber products, and some branches of textiles.[5]

Interest costs too are generally of limited importance in the overall cost structure, at 1.9 per cent of total manufacturing costs and less in most industries.[6] But interest charges accounted for more than 10 per cent of costs in the indigenous branches of metals and basic industrial chemicals, and between 3.5 and 10 per cent in non-metallic mineral products, rubber products, and some branches of textiles.

Clearly there is a large overlap between the energy-intensive group of industries and those with high interest costs, because energy intensity generally implies capital intensity, and major capital investments usually require significant borrowings. The combined impact of relatively high energy and interest costs in a number of sectors, therefore, makes for a rather distinctive cost structure, which differs significantly from most industries. An extreme example in 1983 was the indigenous branch of basic industrial chemicals, in which energy and interest together accounted for 26.6 per cent of total costs, compared with 5.3 per cent in all manufacturing.

CONCLUSION

To conclude, it is evident that there is a good deal of variation between the cost structures of industries, so that competitive advantages or disadvantages with respect to particular cost items have different implications for different sectors. This is one reason why the performance of industries or firms can vary substantially within a common cost environment. It must be acknowledged, however, that costs are only part of the story of what determines competitiveness. Quality of management and the other non-cost or non-price factors can also play a crucial role. Consequently, it is common to find that different firms in the same general line of business within a common cost environment differ considerably in their degree of competitive success.

Notes

1. Industrial Development Authority, *The Irish Economy Expenditures of the Irish Manufacturing Sector*, Dublin: IDA 1985.
2. The difference between 'Labour costs' in column 2 of table 3.1 and 'Wages and salaries' in column 1 is 4.8 per cent. But this would be slightly inaccurate as an estimate of non-wage labour costs, since the two data sets are for different years and have somewhat

different coverage. The CSO's 1984 *Census of Industrial Enterprises* gives a figure for 'other labour costs', apart from wages and salaries, of about 3 per cent of industrial *turnover*.

3. See, for example, Confederation of Irish Industry, *CII Newsletter*, vol. 47, no. 21 (1987); Department of Industry and Commerce, *Review of Industrial Performance, 1986*, Dublin: Stationery Office (Pl. 4769) 1987; Colm McCarthy, 'Industrial Costs and Industrial Policy' (paper read to Dublin Economics Workshop conference), 1986.
4. The cost of liability and commercial property insurance for *business* in 1986 was £224 million, according to the *CII Newsletter* (see note 3). If the share of this total borne by the manufacturing sector was in proportion to its employment, it came to £60 million, or 0.5 per cent of manufacturing sales; or if manufacturing is assumed to have borne half of total business insurance costs, it would amount to 0.9 per cent of manufacturing sales.
5. Central Statistics Office, *Census of Industrial Production, 1984*, Dublin: Stationery Office (Pl. 5235) 1987.
6. See note 1.

COMPETITIVENESS AND OUTPUT: WHAT EMPIRICAL MODELS SHOW

John Bradley

Economic and Social Research Institute

4

In a small open economy like Ireland's, with its almost uniquely high ratio of exports to GNP, the issue of international competitiveness is obviously of serious concern. A severe loss of competitiveness occurred during the period 1977–80 and was the subject of an important Government-sponsored report.[1] The object of the report was to measure and evaluate this loss and to recommend a 'norm' for domestic cost increases in the future, which, with the implementation of appropriate incomes and other policies, would arrest the loss in competitiveness. While the report provided a clear exposition of methods of defining and measuring competitiveness, it highlighted the unsatisfactory nature of the empirical evidence. Little clear evidence was produced to quantify the mechanisms whereby the competitiveness loss explained the stagnation of activity and shedding of jobs in the industrial sector and elsewhere in the economy.

Recently loss of competitiveness has again become an important issue, and OECD figures show that while competitiveness with respect to the EMS countries has stabilised and is now improving, a rapid loss with respect to the UK has occurred since 1986 (see chapter 7).

The purpose of this chapter is to re-examine empirical evidence on the role of competitiveness in the light of work on economic modelling that has been carried out since the 1981 report was published. To execute this task properly requires us first to take a view on how the Irish industrial sector functions both in isolation and in its relationship with the rest of the economy. We discuss such a framework below with a view to isolating some important elements in the analysis of competitiveness. Such elements include the reasons why multinational firms choose to locate manufacturing activity in Ireland rather than elsewhere; the sensitivity of industrial employment to wages; the extent to which capital can be substituted for labour if labour costs rise relative to the cost of machines; and the factors influencing the determination of wage increases. Within the industrial sector, the distinction between indigenous industries and the newer multinationals is also of consequence. Outside the industrial sector the influence of the non-traded or sheltered sectors on industrial competitiveness is important, and includes the role of marketed services, Government expenditure, and taxation policies.

Recent developments in economic theory have provided a complex array of possible explanations of how economies function (Barry provides a lucid guide to theories appropriate for analysis in Ireland[2]). The particular value of formal mathematical and statistical models is that they help to isolate assumptions that are crucial to any particular approach. Empirical (or econometric) work attempts to test theories against the actual historical outcome and provides some quantification of the key channels of influence that are of policy importance. Below we outline a possible approach to the empirical study of the Irish industrial sector, and attempt to quantify the mechanisms through which changes in competitiveness originate and affect output, employment, and investment.

We also examine the implications of three ways in which Irish competitiveness can improve. These involve an autonomous deterioration in world competitiveness (a benign, if unrealistic, scenario for Ireland); a cut in indirect taxation; and a cut in public sector employment. We use the ESRI medium-term economic model to explore the impact on the economy of these changes. Such a model cannot be entirely uncontroversial, but at least it has the advantage of being a functioning policy model whose structure has been empirically studied, which has been used to produce published forecasts and policy analysis,[3] and which is the subject of systematic review and updating.

Finally, we discuss some areas where further research is being done to deepen our understanding of how changes in competitiveness arise and how they influence the growth and development of the Irish economy.

COMPETITIVENESS: A FRAMEWORK FOR ANALYSIS

At the very centre of the debate on the role of competitiveness in Ireland is that part of the economy that sells a large fraction of its output abroad or produces goods or services for domestic consumption that are the subject of competition from imports.

Let us concentrate on manufacturing industry for the moment. The firms making up this sector consist in part of Irish subsidiaries of foreign multinationals, but also of indigenous firms either based entirely in Ireland or with both Irish and foreign plants. With the progressive dismantling of trade barriers since the Second World War, the obstacles to supplying the world market from plants located in many different countries have largely vanished. The relatively free movement of capital and the free mobility of entrepreneurial talent have meant that the geographical location of firms, and individual plants within firms, is quite flexible. When multinational firms wish to increase production or launch new products, they deal with a market covering many countries. For any given product line they face essentially three choices: *how much* to produce; *where* to produce it, among a wide range of alternative countries or regions within countries; and *how* to produce it, i.e. having chosen a specific location, what technology is to be used in production. These are clearly interrelated decisions, but it is useful to isolate them, in this order.

Since we are looking at this process from the point of view of Ireland, we may be permitted to omit from our analysis the first choice—how much to plan to produce for the global market—by invoking the concept of a given world demand over which Ireland has no influence. The second choice—where to produce—involves a decision on where to locate a plant, or, if the plant is already in place, what portion of world demand is to be serviced from it. Given easily transferable technology and capital between regions, the decision to locate productive capacity in one region rather than another will be based mainly on factors such as labour costs, profitability, tax regimes, and transport costs. (Some of these factors constitute the measures of relative competitiveness outlined in chapter 2.)

Attempts to capture the empirical relationship between location and cost can either examine how Ireland's share of world mobile *investment* is related to relative competitiveness measures or how our share of world *productive capacity* (i.e. output capacity) is determined. Of course there are major problems in arriving at a suitable measure of the 'world' against which we compete. For example, increased profitability of American firms tends to encourage them to locate subsidiary production plants in Ireland and/or to increase utilisation of existing Irish plants to service European markets, and to benefit from Ireland's EEC access and our advantageous corporate tax regime. However, increased industrial profitability in Spain, Portugal, Belgium, regions of the UK, etc., tends to attract such multinational investment away from Ireland. Hence the 'world' consists of 'source' countries, which provide multinational investment if they are doing well in their own economies, and 'sink' countries, which bid away this investment from Ireland if they are too competitive with us. In empirical work at present we are forced by lack of data to use the competitiveness of a group of the largest OECD economies as representative of the 'world' with which Ireland competes.

In considering Irish industrial competitiveness, attention is normally concentrated on comparisons of wage costs and unit labour costs. However, a wide range of other elements affect competitiveness, including the cost of domestically produced inputs, for example electricity, other services, and interest rates. The best indicator of overall competitiveness is profitability.

In Ireland this indicator has the additional advantage (which more traditional measures lack) of capturing the effects of the potential for transfer pricing as a factor attracting foreign investment to Ireland. If profitability is defined as the share of added value going to 'capital' (essentially added value less the wage bill), then Ireland's share of world capacity is found to be positively related to relative profitability. An empirical relationship between Ireland's capacity output share and our industrial profitability relative to the 'world' has proved fairly robust. It is found that a 1 per cent gain in competitiveness (as measured by profitability) leads eventually to a 0.4 per cent gain in capacity output share, but that the short-run gain is much smaller.

Having planned the optimum share of world capacity it intends to locate in Ireland, the firm must then make a decision on the nature of the production technology, i.e. how the capital, labour and material inputs are to be best combined to produce this desired output. This leads to relationships in which demands for the different factor inputs are specified as functions of output and of factor input prices. What emerges from empirical work is that Irish factor demands are only moderately sensitive to *Irish* factor prices. For example, ignoring the effects on competitiveness (dealt with above), a 1 per cent rise in the price of labour relative to capital leads eventually to a less than 0.5 per cent fall in the demand for labour. The value for the United States or for other large economies would be nearer unity.[4]

The reason for this low elasticity is that substitution of capital for labour normally takes place through the installation of new plant, a process that often involves the possibility of a change in the production location. The smaller the economy, the more likely it is that factor substitution will involve a shift in productive capacity to other countries, in other words that capital will not replace labour in the Irish factory but will instead seek out lower labour costs in other countries. In larger economies, it is more likely that relocation will take place *within* the large country, leaving national output capacity unchanged. (Regional reallocation will, of course, occur, for example the shift in the United States to the sun-belt states from the industrial north.) The movement of fixed investment and production capacity to locations where the highest profits are to be made provides an important channel for transmitting the effects of international competitiveness shifts, a channel not well identified by more traditional statistics on international economic linkages.

In summary, a high rate of profit in Ireland encourages domestic firms to expand and foreign firms to locate new activities in Ireland. However, if labour costs are high relative to the cost of capital, such growth will be capital-intensive and create little employment.

Since domestic wage costs are the most obvious element of profitability that can change in the short run, domestic wage bargaining institutions take on much more importance than in larger, less open economies. Industrial wage rates are the outcome of bargaining between unions and employers, with the frequent intervention of the Government. Having worked through the formalised theory of such bargaining,[5] we arrive at expressions that determine wage rates as functions of at least four explanatory variables: output prices; the 'wedge' between the wage denominated in output prices and the take-home consumption wage actually enjoyed by workers; the rate of unemployment; and labour productivity. The price that the producer can obtain for his product clearly influences the price at which he can profitably purchase factor inputs, particularly labour. The 'wedge' effect arises because workers try to bargain in terms of a take-home wage denominated in consumer prices and not in terms of gross pre-tax wages. The unemployment effect has come to be called the Phillips curve; it basically states that the more people who are unemployed in an economy, the lower will be the subsequent wage demands from those still with jobs. The productivity effect comes from workers' efforts to maintain their share of added value: that is, they want to enjoy at least some of the gains from higher output per person.

Empirical analysis shows that in the short term (i.e. within one year) the following is the effect on wages of a specified change in each of the above explanatory variables (Bradley gives details[6]):

1 per cent rise in producer prices:	1 per cent rise in wage rate
1 per cent rise in the 'wedge':	0.55 per cent rise in wage rate
1 percentage point rise in unemployment rate:	2.3 per cent *fall* in wage rate
1 per cent rise in labour productivity:	0.65 per cent rise in wage rate

In the context of an isolated relationship, it is not completely meaningful to look at long-run effects, since the explanatory variables are interrelated with each other in a complete model.

Average annual earnings in industry rose by 104 per cent over the period 1980–87. As a rough guide, let us consider how much of this increase is accounted for by each of the explanatory terms:

EXPLANATORY VARIABLE	PERCENTAGE RISE IN PERIOD 1980–87	CONTRIBUTION TO WAGE INFLATION	
		SHORT-RUN	LONG-RUN
Output prices	38.0 per cent	38.0 per cent (+)	38.0 per cent (+)
Tax wedge	50.7 per cent	27.9 per cent (+)	45.0 per cent (+)
Unemployment rate	11.2 percentage points	25.8 per cent (–)	39.0 per cent (–)
Labour productivity	60.0 per cent	39.0 per cent (+)	60.0 per cent (+)

Note that the long-run contribution of prices, the tax wedge and unemployment are approximately equal in magnitude. By far the largest long-run contribution comes from labour productivity increases. In some ways this is an Irish example of the phenomenon called the 'Dutch disease', where the high-technology and high-productivity firms (mostly foreign-owned) give large wage increases, which they can afford because of their high levels of profitability. This tends to bid up wages in the low-technology, low-productivity firms (largely indigenous and labour-intensive), a process further exacerbated by nation-wide pay agreements and 'understandings'. The low-productivity firms tend to get squeezed out in the process due to their lower levels of profitability.

FIG. 4.1 **Measures of Competitiveness**

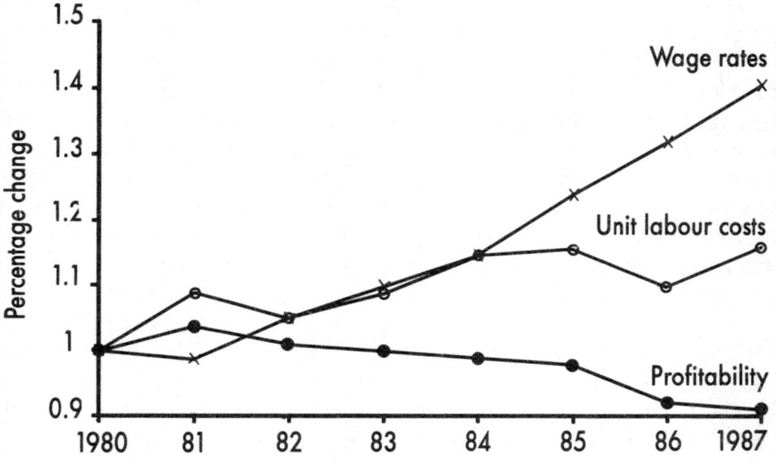

How has Irish competitiveness evolved over the recent past? In fig. 4.1 we show movements in the best available measure of competitiveness—relative profitability—as well as movements in more 'traditional' measures, i.e. relative average annual earnings and unit labour costs. All are relative to a suitably weighted average of the main OECD economies. On the basis of the relative earnings measure, there has been some loss in competitiveness. Using relative unit labour costs we see a gain of 15 per cent; using relative profitability we see a gain of 40 per cent. This latter measure provides a good explanation of the expansion of Irish industrial capacity, but this expansion, being concentrated in a few sectors (computers, pharmaceuticals, electrical and instrument engineering), has not provided commensurate aggregate employment growth, either directly or indirectly through downstream activities.

If we assume that the 10 per cent corporate tax rate in manufacturing is not to be further lowered, to what extent can 'profitability' competitiveness be influenced by policy? This essentially requires policies that influence wage inflation. Looking at each of the determinants of wage inflation, the output price is set in foreign markets and is only very partially under domestic control. The 'wedge' can be directly influenced by Government taxation and subsidy policies. The unemployment rate is influenced both by domestic factors (public sector job creation, private sector employment, emigration) and international factors (the state of world activity). The underlying rate of productivity growth is determined by the structure of industrial growth, established work practices, and the quantity and age of the capital stock. Hence only the 'wedge' and the unemployment rate are in any way amenable to policy influence in the short term.

Here the real dilemma of Irish industrial growth becomes apparent. The direct benefit to the Irish economy from multinational enterprises consists in the wages paid to Irish workers directly employed, the national product indirectly generated in the domestic industrial and market services sectors, and any taxes paid on profits. From this must be netted off the costs of attracting these firms to Ireland (capital grants, training grants, and other promotional activities). Research has shown that the multinationals tend to be fairly capital and R&D-intensive, obtain most of their inputs abroad, have relatively weak downstream links with the rest of the economy, and repatriate the greater part of their profits. Since their principal benefit to the Irish economy consists in the wages they pay to workers, attempting to raise competitiveness by lowering wages reduces that benefit, with potentially little gain in competitiveness. However, the effects on employment in *traditional* firms of the high wages in the multinational sector being transmitted through to the rest of the economy can be critical. The net results of these interacting influences are explored in the next section.

OUTPUT, EMPLOYMENT, AND COMPETITIVENESS: A MODEL-BASED ANALYSIS

We turn now to the examination of the effects of competitiveness gains on employment and output, and use the ESRI model of the Irish economy to carry out some experiments. The industrial sector of this model is constructed along the lines outlined above. However, the model also has a marketed services sector, where output is driven by domestic demand, prices are simply a mark-up on costs, and where, given its large self-employment component, the investment/labour ratio is less sensitive to relative factor prices than is industry. However, an important link between the industrial and services sectors is the fact that the rate of industrial wage inflation is passed on to services, in other words the labour market is assumed to be fairly homogeneous. Conversely, any wage inflation in services that is in excess of the industrial rate will bring upward pressure on industrial wages through the effect of driving up the 'wedge' variable in the industrial wage equation, thus causing a loss of international competitiveness.

The model also has a Government sector, where tax rates and expenditures are set. Direct and indirect tax cuts drive down the 'wedge' between pay rates denominated in product and take-home consumer prices, thus moderating wage inflation. Public sector employment cuts drive up the unemployment rate and, through the Phillips curve, put downward pressure on wages in the private and public sectors.

In our experiments we look at three sources of competitiveness gain. First, we simply assume that, in a *deus ex machina* fashion, the 'world' profit rate falls by 10 per cent below an assumed bench-mark path for the years 1988–92. This could come about, for example, if certain countries that compete with Ireland for internationally mobile investment raised their corporate tax rates substantially, or if Irish factor productivity were to improve autonomously. The effects from this experiment will feed directly into the Irish economy through the industrial sector.

The other two sources are related to domestic policy decisions. In one we cut the rate of VAT permanently by one percentage point below the bench-mark value. Here the gain in competitiveness originates in the 'wedge' effect on wage bargaining. In the other we cut public sector employment by 1,000. Here, if no tax rates are changed, the gain in competitiveness arises through the Phillips curve effect in the wage equation.

The bench-mark used in the experiments is that presented in the most recent ESRI *Medium-Term Review*, that for 1987–92, where full details are provided. In order to interpret the outcome of the experiments it is necessary to realise that a process of tax and public expenditure indexation is used that keeps the *real* tax burden and the *real* level of expenditure programmes fixed at 1988 levels, no matter what price changes result from the experiments. The two important exceptions relate to public sector employment and wage rates. The employment cuts proposed in the autumn 1987 estimates are implemented in 1988–89, and employment is subsequently frozen at the 1989 level up to 1992. The public sector pay agreement is also strictly implemented, so that the rate of public sector wage cost inflation is fixed for 1988–90 (at 6.3, 4.5 and 4.2 per cent, respectively) and linked to industrial wage inflation for 1991–92. Hence, the policy stance is the one anticipated at the time of writing.

Case 1: The External Profit Rate Shock The immediate impact of an *ex ante* 10 per cent gain in Irish competitiveness causes an increase in employment (fig. 4.2) and output (fig. 4.5) in the industrial sector. While small in the first year, the gain rises to over 10,000 jobs by 1989–90. In the case of output, the gain rises to over 2 per cent. This increase in employment tends to drive up industrial wage rates through the unemployment (Phillips curve) effect by almost 5 per cent by 1991 (fig. 4.4). The initial *ex ante* 10 per cent improvement in

10 PER CENT SUSTAINED EX-ANTE FALL IN WORLD PROFITABILITY

FIG. 4.2 **Sectoral Employment Changes Deviations from Bench-mark**

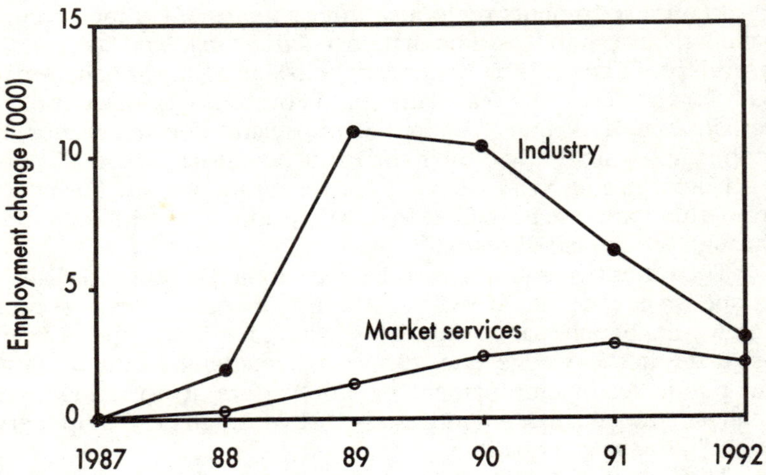

FIG. 4.3 **Irish Industrial Profitability Deviation from Bench-mark (%)**

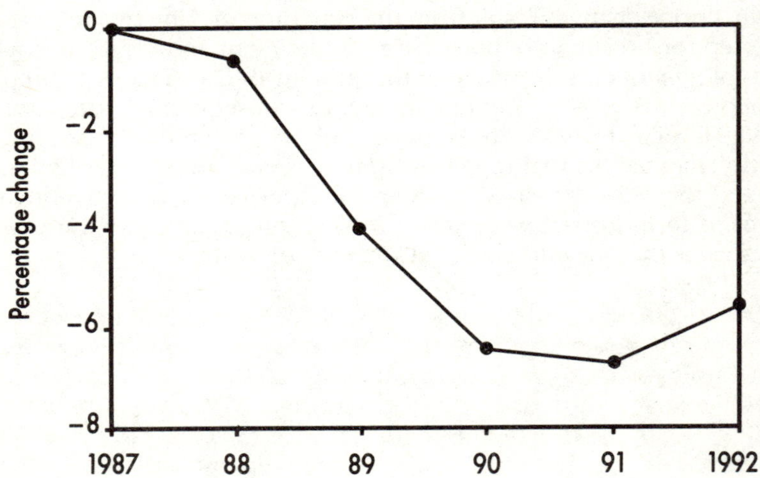

FIG. 4.4

Wage and Price Inflation
Deviation from Bench-mark

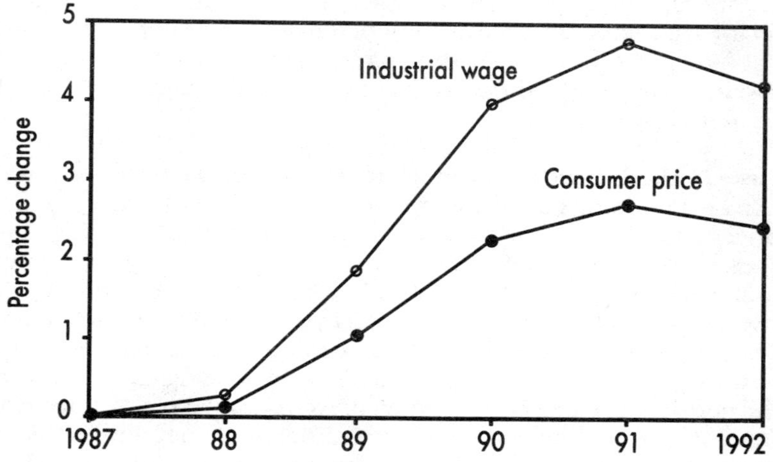

FIG. 4.5

Sectoral Output Effects
Deviations from Bench-mark

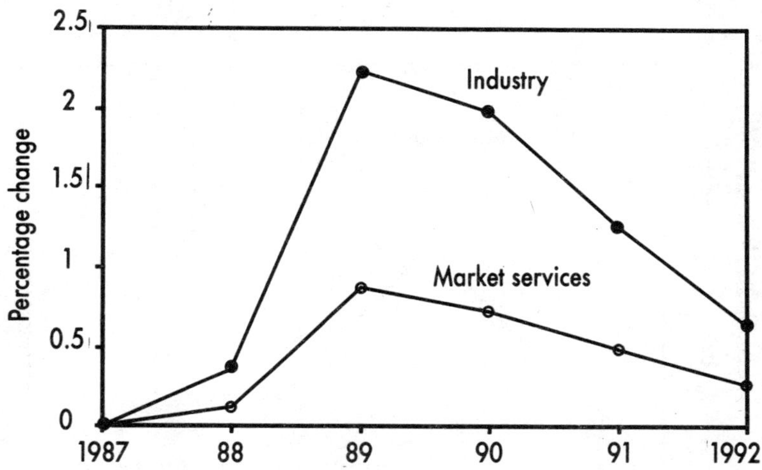

Irish competitiveness is gradually whittled away by increasing labour costs (fig 4.3), so that by 1990–91 almost 7 percentage points have been lost. Meanwhile, the marketed services sector has been enjoying a more gentle improvement, dampened to some extent by the public sector wage policy in force in the bench-mark for the period 1988–90. In both cases the economy shows a strong tendency to react in such a way as to negate the shock, so that by 1992 the remaining real effects are relatively small.

Case 2: The Indirect Tax Cut Here, the immediate impact of the 1 percentage point cut in the VAT rate is to drive down consumer prices and, through the 'wedge', to drive down wage rates (fig. 4.8). Marketed services benefit most, where the employment gain amounts to almost 2,000 jobs by 1990–92 and comes about mainly through the rise in private consumption, induced by a rise in disposable income. The output gain is almost 0.5 of a percentage point immediately, and remains at that level to 1992. Here, the gain is being exaggerated by the public sector pay policy, which prevents public sector wage rates from falling in line with the lower inflation and thus reducing consumption. In addition, since public sector expenditure and tax

1 Percentage Point Permanent Cut in the VAT Rate

FIG. 4.6

Sectoral Employment Changes
Deviations from Bench-mark

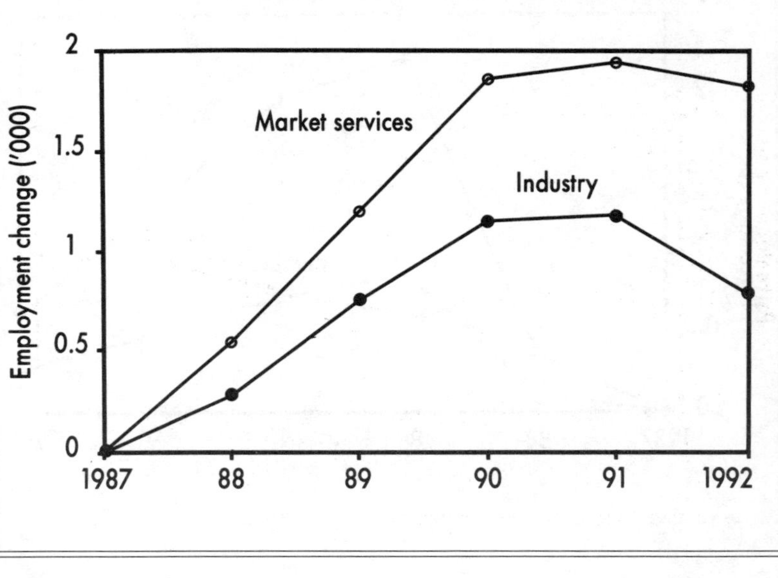

FIG. 4.7

Irish Industrial Profitability
Deviation from Bench-mark

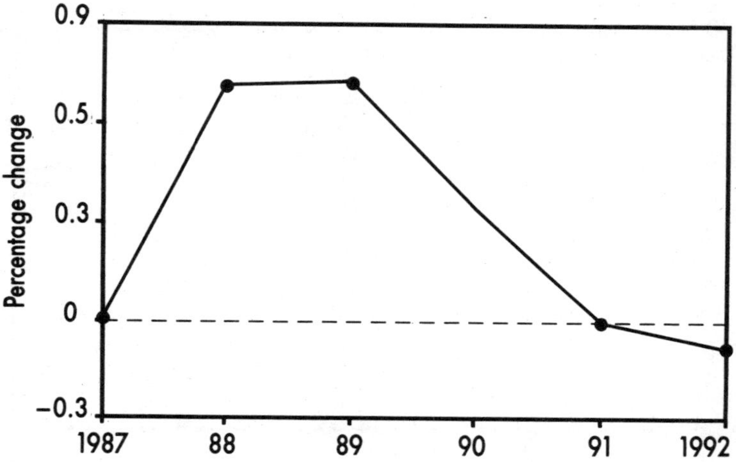

FIG. 4.8

Wage and Price Inflation
Deviation from Bench-mark

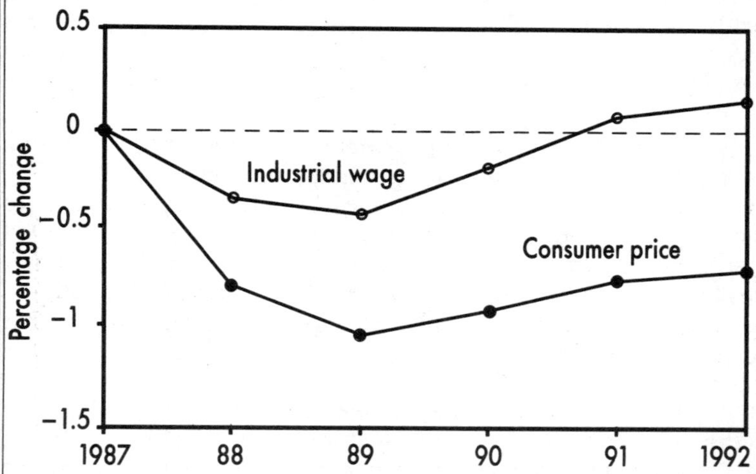

FIG 4.9 Sectoral Output Effects Deviation from Bench-mark

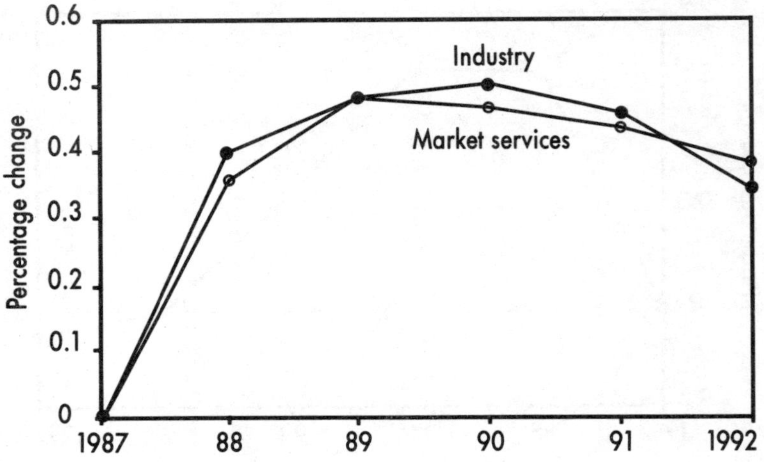

rates are maintained in real terms beyond 1988, any net loss of tax revenue is simply made up by accumulating national debt rather than deflating domestic demand. Meanwhile in the industry sector there has been a gain in profitability of over 0.7 per cent by 1988–89, but a steady movement back to the initial rate by 1991 (fig. 4.7). This induces a gain of over 1,000 jobs by 1990–91 and a gain in output almost identical to that in marketed services (fig. 4.9).

Case 3: The Public Sector Employment Cut The effect of cutting 1,000 public sector jobs initially increases numbers unemployed by 1,000. The subsequent loosening of the labour market begins to drive down wage inflation through the Phillips curve (fig. 4.12). By 1989 industrial wages are down by almost 0.4 per cent, and consumer prices have started to drift down as well. The gain in profitability in industry (fig. 4.11) drives up industrial employment (fig. 4.10), so that by 1991 almost 600 jobs have been gained and output is up by over 0.1 per cent (fig. 4.13). The market services sector is relatively unaffected, since two competing influences are at work: the domestic deflation of the reduction in public sector jobs, and the induced boost transmitted from the industrial sector. So, by 1992 about 700 jobs have been gained in the private sector as a result of the cut of 1,000 in public sector jobs.

Cut of 1,000 Jobs in the Public Sector

FIG. 4.10

Sectoral Employment Changes Deviations from Bench-mark

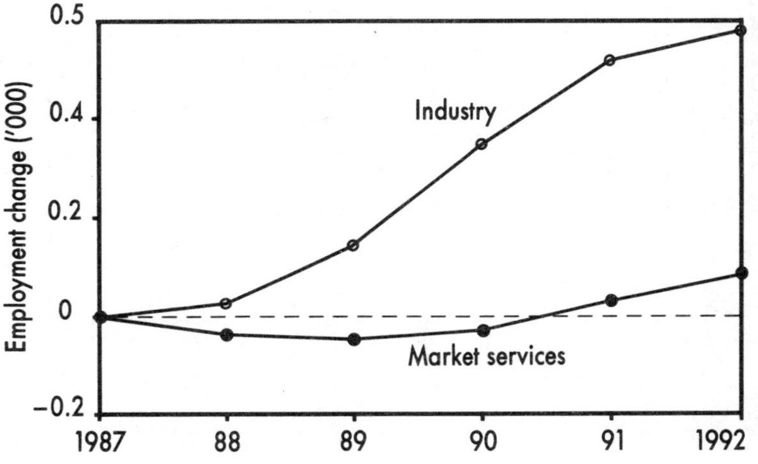

FIG. 4.11

Irish Industrial Profitability Deviation from Bench-mark

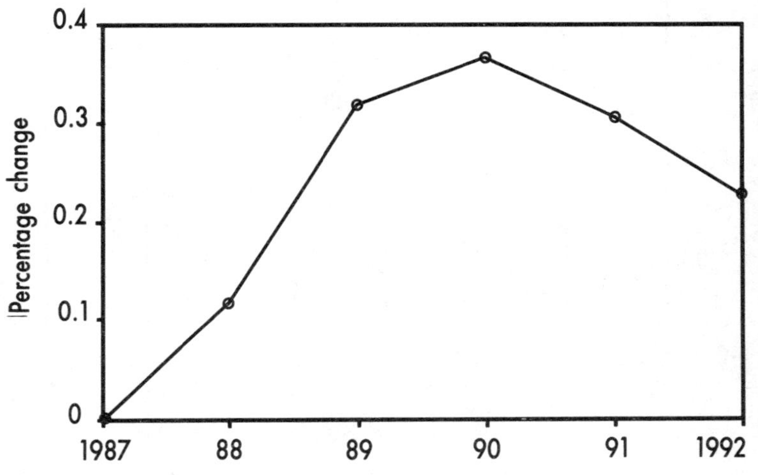

FIG. 4.12

Wage and Price Inflation
Deviation from Bench-mark

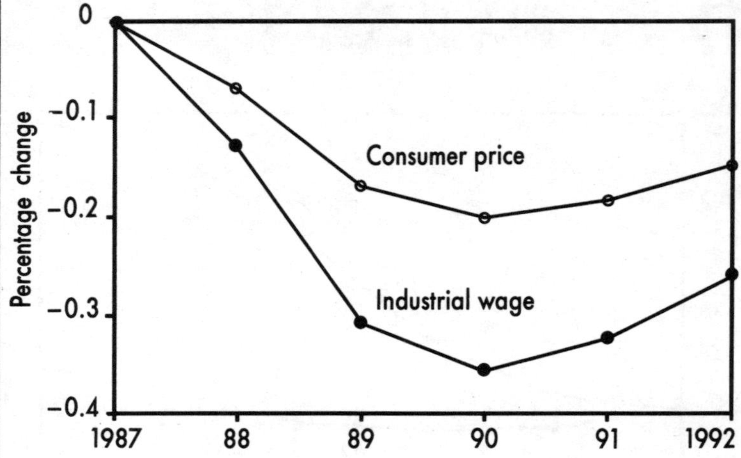

FIG. 4.13

Sectoral Output Effects
Deviation from Bench-mark

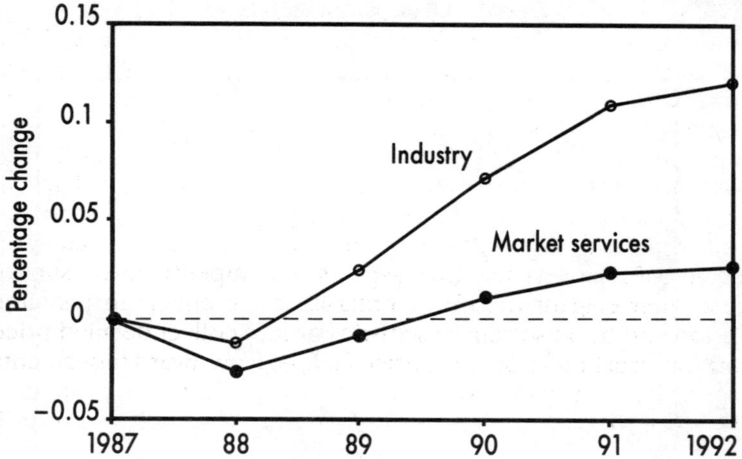

CONCLUSIONS AND SOME UNRESOLVED ISSUES

The above experiments confirm the expectation that cost competitiveness does matter and that a gain in competitiveness always results in increased jobs in the private sector. Moreover, the maintenance of cost competitiveness is not just a matter for strict pay discipline in the exposed industrial sector. The public sector can, by cutting taxes and/or reducing publicly funded employment, induce wage moderation in the industrial sector through the 'wedge' and Phillips curve effects. Such downward wage pressure should, in theory, be partially dampened by the decreased flow of public services arising from any reduced state activity, but these effects are difficult to detect empirically. The opposite case, i.e. greater pay moderation in exchange for increased state services, also seems to be weak or absent (a 'begrudger' phenomenon perhaps?). Similarly, the sheltered sectors can, if wage settlements are moderate, pass on this reduced pressure on wages to the exposed sector, through lower consumer price inflation.

Needless to say, the present model can be elaborated and developed in many ways. However, with existing data it is nearly impossible to split out and study the important sub-components of the industrial sector, i.e. new high-technology foreign-owned manufacturing, indigenous low-technology manufacturing, utilities, and the construction industry. To do this would require data covering a long enough period to permit accurate statistical calculations. Similarly, it is difficult to isolate and quantify the links between industry and marketed services, since the most comprehensive available picture of the economy that might permit this refers to 1975 (the year of the most recent CSO input-output table). There is enough circumstantial evidence to indicate that these links are weak and that the industries that are attracted here by the expectation of high after-tax profitability remain as 'enclaves' and create a disappointing amount of downstream activity in the domestic economy.

Even analysis along these lines is of its nature very partial and incomplete. It is easy to overemphasise the role of wage moderation in restoring previously lost competitiveness (this theme is taken up in the following chapters). Perhaps economic modellers are fixated on the details of relatively marginal aspects of competitiveness, simply because their elegant theories emphasise price effects in resource allocation and because central statistics offices collect detailed price and output data but ignore non-price factors. Downward movements in wage inflation may merely make our industry more competitive in the short run for goods which, in a longer-term perspective, have little potential for market expansion. The vital aspects of marketing, quality, design and reliability are probably best tackled directly, particularly in an economy with substantial migration flows. Nevertheless, in the short to medium term, increased competitiveness through the means of lower wage costs would appear to be one avenue towards a resumption of economic growth and could perhaps provide breathing-space during which the more fundamental non-price problems in the economy are tackled.

Notes

1. T. Baker, D. McAleese, and B. M. Walsh, *Report of the Committee on Costs and Competitiveness,* Dublin: Stationery Office (Pl. 154), 1981.
2. F. Barry, 'Macroeconomic Perspectives on Irish Unemployment' in *Perspectives on Economic Policy,* Dublin: Centre for Economic Research, UCD, 1987.
3. J. Bradley, J. Fitzgerald, and R. A. Storey, *Medium-Term Review, 1987–1992,* Dublin: Economic and Social Research Institute 1987.
4. J. Bradley and J. Fitzgerald, 'Industrial Output and Factor Input Determination in an Econometric Model of a Small Open Economy' in *European Economic Review,* vol. 32 (1988), 1227–41.
5. M. Andrews and S. J. Nickel, 'Unions, Real Wages and Employment in Britain, 1951–79' in *Oxford Economic Papers,* vol. 35 (supplement) (1983), 183–206.
6. J. Bradley, 'Wages, Taxation, Unemployment and Productivity: the Irish Phillips Curve Re-examined', Dublin: Economic and Social Research Institute 1988.

MARKET STRATEGIES, COMPETITIVENESS, AND GROWTH

Charles Carroll

Irish Management Institute

5

In this chapter we direct our attention mainly to the question of market share. How important is market share within any competitiveness framework? In spite of the considerable controversy that surrounds the issue, the most important empirical evidence still supports the view that market share is very strongly associated with financial performance. We examine the implications of this conclusion for the competitiveness of a small country such as Ireland that must address seemingly big international markets.

Two aspects of the problem are of concern:

(a) Setting meaningful criteria for deciding which type of market sectors are attractive to Ireland's small-scale industry;

(b) Deciding how best to gain an 'adequate' market share within such sectors.

We have drawn mainly on our experience with the Profit Impact of Market Strategy (PIMS) programme members to help throw light on these central strategic questions. Any growth in Ireland's industrial base, together with the resulting benefits in wealth and jobs, depends on the nature of the answers to these questions.

DOES MARKET SHARE STILL MATTER?

The most recent reviews of the business implications of market share continue to support the proposition that market share remains a factor of major importance in determining whether a business will have poor, mediocre or superior financial performance (and therefore, by implication, the ability to push further growth and development). Gale and Buzzell reviewed the controversy that continues to surround the issue since the 1960s.[1] They concluded that the main counter-arguments against the importance of market share do not stand up against the most powerful sources of empirical evidence.

Earlier company-level studies in the United States show a very significant and robust relationship between market share and profitability, although the studies did also show that the magnitude of that relationship was contingent on the presence of many other factors.[2] More recent studies of the US Federal Trade Commission data for 'Lines of Business' have confirmed these earlier conclusions.[3] These studies have also tended to discount the idea that the relationship between market share and profitability is spurious, that is, the relationship is really a function of some other factor or factors. Even when the studies include a control for numerous other factors, market share still emerges as a factor of major importance.

The most important other source of single and multivariate studies of market share has been the PIMS data-base, which in 1988 contained a rich array of data on about three thousand 'business units' drawn from across North America and Europe.

FIG. 5.1

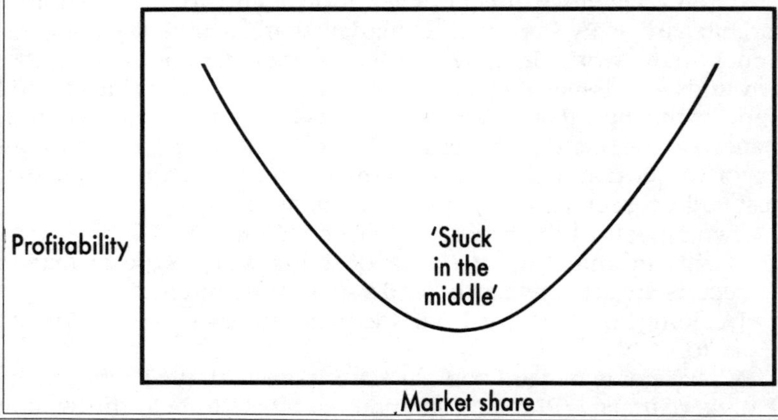

Before we examine the PIMS findings it is worth reviewing the most common objections to the 'importance of market share' thesis. For example, the influence of Michael Porter has been important in suggesting that the relationship between market share and returns is really a U shape (see fig. 5.1).[4]

Porter suggests that two kinds of business make money: those that are very dominant in their markets, and those that are small. The place *not* to be is 'stuck in the middle'. This perspective seems to contradict flatly the more 'straight-line' relationship depicted by PIMS and other research studies. It also conforms to the plain man's view that many 'small' businesses do make money—in many cases seeming to outperform 'big' businesses.

It should be remembered, however, that Porter's analysis is an 'industry-wide' market share analysis. The small business may be small in the industry but big in a sub-sector of the industry. Alternatively, there may well be small businesses which, in spite of the odds or because of the presence of other contingent factors, do in fact achieve superior financial performance. Common sense suggests that, undoubtedly, there are. However, a few swallows don't make a summer. Porter relies too much on small samples and particular cases to support his assertions. Such large-scale industry-wide studies as do exist (for example the FTC 'Lines of Business') flatly contradict his main thesis.

FIG 5.2

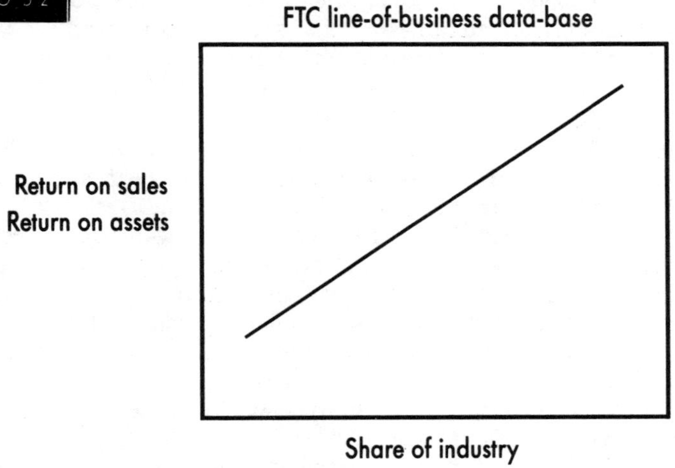

More recently, the Boston Consulting Group, a one-time proponent of the pursuit of market dominance, drew back from the strong emphasis on market share as a strategic factor. In a new attempt to classify strategic environments the BCG suggested that market share mattered strongly only in volume markets but not in the three other categories.[5]

FIG 5.3

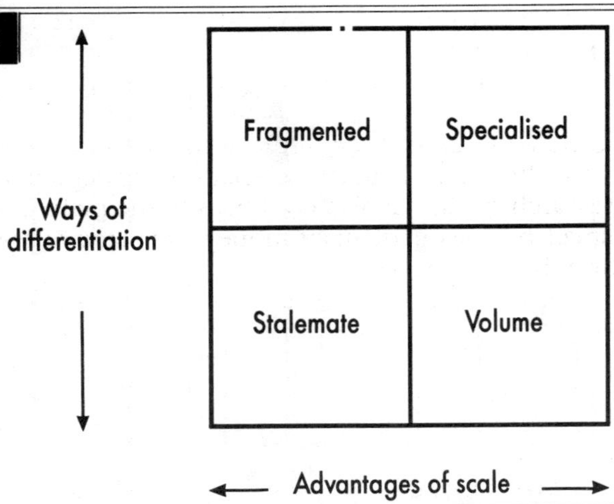

However, this contention does not stand up to evidence either. Internal studies of the PIMS data, which replicated each of the four environments, revealed that the ROI/market share relationship was as strong as ever, though it did vary with each environment.

THE PIMS FINDINGS ON BUSINESS UNITS

Arguably, if we are to uncover the implications of competitive position and its determinants we must study competition where it actually happens, that is to say, in discrete market settings where rival products meet one another head on with their relative efforts in product, service, pricing and promotional efforts.

Arguably, 'countries' don't compete with one another. Even 'companies' don't compete with one another: only their business units do, within the relevant served market categories. The PIMS researchers have sought to construct a large body of observed experience of this kind. Particular attention has been paid to gathering data about market share and the relative position of competitors. Any measure of market share raises the related question of the market 'scope' of any particular business, i.e. the question, 'market share of what market?' Which set of customers or which set of customer requirements is the business trying to serve, in the sense of making a serious marketing effort to do so? Thus a business may choose to address only the 'household' end of the market and opt not to call on organisational buyers. It makes sense to measure market share only of that part of the market being served.

FIG. 5.4

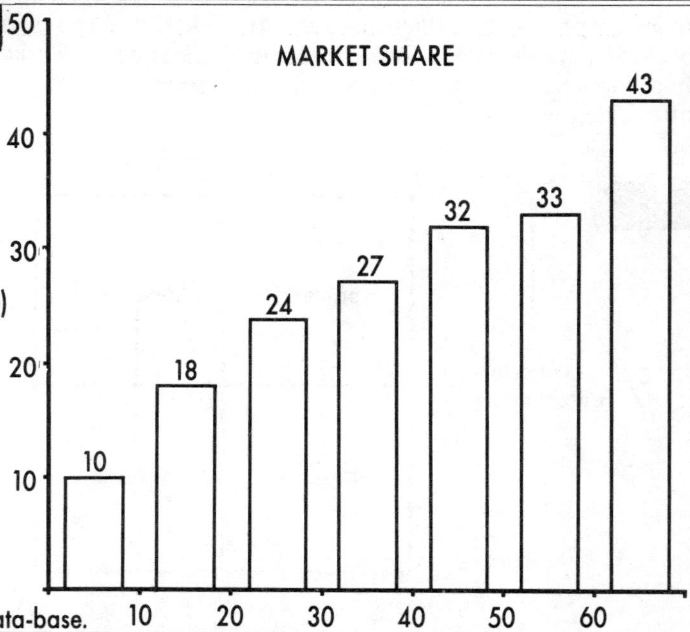

Source:
PIMS data-base.

The main findings of PIMS can be set out in terms of the very strong, positive relationship between ROI (%) (after-tax, pre-interest) and four different measures of market position:

(a) Market share (%) (i.e. sales/served market (%)) (fig. 5.4);
(b) Market rank;
(c) Relative market domination (sales times sales of leading competitor);
(d) Relative market share (%) (sales/combined sales of three leading competitors (%)).

The main reasons advanced to explain this relationship usually relate to cost position. Businesses with larger-volume throughput than their rivals usually have better economies of scale in procurement, manufacturing, and distribution, and in important tactical muscles such as research and development, marketing, and management. Whatever the detailed reasons, the phenomenon is very powerful and robust.

IMPLICATIONS FOR IRELAND

At first sight the implications for Ireland of the PIMS finding on market share is very pessimistic and perhaps goes a long way towards explaining the poor financial performance of Ireland's indigenous trading sector. In spite of well-known exceptions (such as Bailey's Irish Cream, Waterford Glass), Ireland's market position in many important international markets can be depicted as weak or marginal. There is evidence that in two of its most important product or market areas—food products in the UK[6] and tourism generally[7]—Ireland has even experienced a slide in market shares.

Too often we hear export policies enunciated that say, 'There are huge markets abroad. If my company can get 1 per cent of a big foreign market that will treble my turnover. Very quickly most of my output will be exported.' Such a policy focus can look good at first and appear to improve the country's aggregate export performance. It looks good in the national accounts. But for the individual business it can be a strategic trap. One per cent of any market, however big, will usually not yield an adequate return. Rivals may tolerate a small Irish presence as long as tides are rising. But with the onset of a slowdown they may be quick to use their experience and size to crush small-scale competitors.

An alternative policy that is frequently advocated is that Irish companies should *focus* their efforts to identify a unique niche, and then seek to dominate that niche. This sounds a sensible idea and seems to address the market-share dilemma. There are problems, however. Niche strategies require a lot of sophistication, for example in the analysis of information and in the disciplined execution of such a policy. Both characteristics are often lacking in small-scale Irish companies. Also there is evidence that niches offer only short-term protection.[8] They often evaporate quickly in the face of changed circumstances and the action of large industry-wide competitors.

A more promising idea for Irish industry is to focus on more substantial segments where contingent factors render the impact of market share less steep. While not among the leaders in the sector, the business would seek an 'adequate' market share, which, combined with an appropriate mix of other tactics, would yield a higher than expected return. The first component of such a strategy is to make sure that the 'segment' is really a segment, that is to say, a customer set that really does differ significantly in its requirements and preferences and where the economics of supplying the requirements also differ from the rest of the wider industry. Such segments cannot be wished arbitrarily into existence by managers who simply want their businesses redefined as 'adequate-share' instead of 'marginal-share'.

Such segment differences do exist, however, and given that Ireland must focus or specialise and that it cannot attain a large market share, what sector characteristics would be most attractive?

Since economies of scale are an important reason why market share has a big impact, it would be important to avoid sectors with structural cost components in which economies of scale are vital. For example, economies of scale are high in marketing. Sectors that are not *intrinsically* marketing-intensive would be attractive, for example where there are a few big end-use customers and relatively large order sizes. Sectors where value added is modest rather than very high and capital-intensive, are also less vulnerable to scale economies.

These few insights have long suggested to the author that the widespread enthusiasm in Ireland for the idea of creating international-class *consumer* brands is highly questionable. On the contrary, they suggest that a far less obtrusive focus on carefully segmented industrial buyers makes much more sense. The author has experience of numerous Irish companies where the shift of effort in this direction resulted in sustained success (for example in dairying and in textiles).

This pessimistic view of Ireland's opportunities in consumer products refers to attempts to build market position from a small, inexperienced starting-point. It does not preclude the idea of purchasing market share of consumer markets through the *acquisition* of consumer goods businesses with potentially significant brand names—or consumer distribution and marketing facilities. In the author's experience, other small European countries, such as Finland, have pursued such policies successfully.

BUILDING MARKET SHARE

Even if we assume that Ireland cannot expect to achieve market dominance in many market sectors, it is still faced with the task of achieving an 'adequate' share: say 10 per cent in any industrial or institutional market. Arguably this issue is at the core of any debate about competitiveness. How do businesses gain and hold market share against their leading market rivals?

There is now growing acceptance that competitiveness is a complex, multifaceted phenomenon. Over-simplistic emphasis on unit costs (particularly labour costs) has been recognised as at best a mere proxy measure and largely a function of the availability and reliability of general economic data.[9] The 1980s have seen a spate of books such as *In Search of Excellence*[10] and *The Winning Performance*,[11] which placed enormous emphasis on numerous non-price and non-cost factors and appeared to dent seriously the previous all-pervasive emphasis on cost competitiveness. But we must be careful: too often the conclusions of these authors are based on a relatively small number of cases, which make any broad generalisations suspect.

The PIMS data represent the most elaborate attempt yet to closely study the dynamics of competition with richer data on non-price factors and with samples that are both large and diverse. Yet it is clear from the data that while a number of broad generalisations are possible and are intuitively sensible, much remains to be explained.

Continuing studies of the PIMS companies lend powerful support to the view that an adequate or large market share is (a) a reward for providing better 'value' to the customer and (b) a means of achieving lower cost. 'Value' has two dimensions that are often lost sight of: *relative* price and *relative* product quality. It is the combination of the two factors that is important. It is very evident from the data that aggressive pricing tactics used as a primary instrument have little apparent effect on market share. Indeed, the PIMS experience would suggest that price should be seen as a performance variable rather than a tactical instrument.

FIG. 5.5

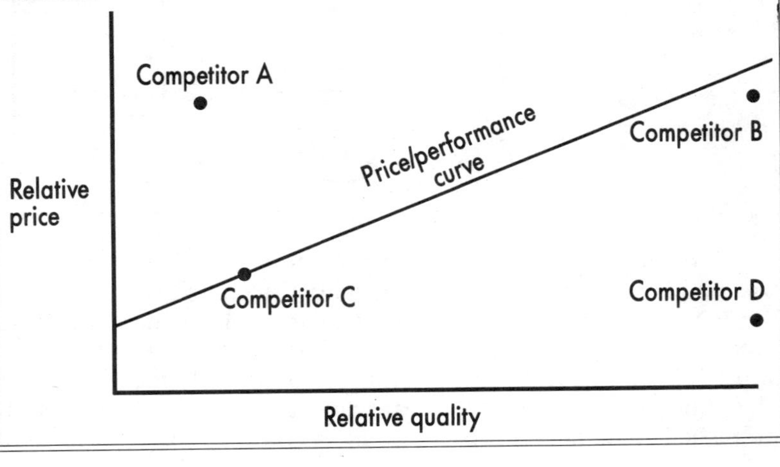

The competitive position of different competitors can be depicted in a 'value map' (see fig. 5.5) of any discrete competitive market. Since we have measures both for relative price and relative quality it is possible to fit a line through the map that provides an indication of what price performance is associated with what level of relative quality.

Businesses falling *on* the line are delivering average value and tend to hold share. Businesses delivering high quality with relative price *below* the price/performance curve are delivering *high* value and tend to gain market share rapidly. Businesses in the opposite situation—delivering poor quality at a high relative price—suffered severe market share losses.

The most surprising result of any examination of these findings is that, *since quality drives market share up, and market share lowers costs, it follows that improving quality lowers costs over time*. The way in which product quality drives competitiveness growth and profitability is depicted in fig. 5.6.

FIG. 5.6 **How Quality Drives Profitability and Growth**

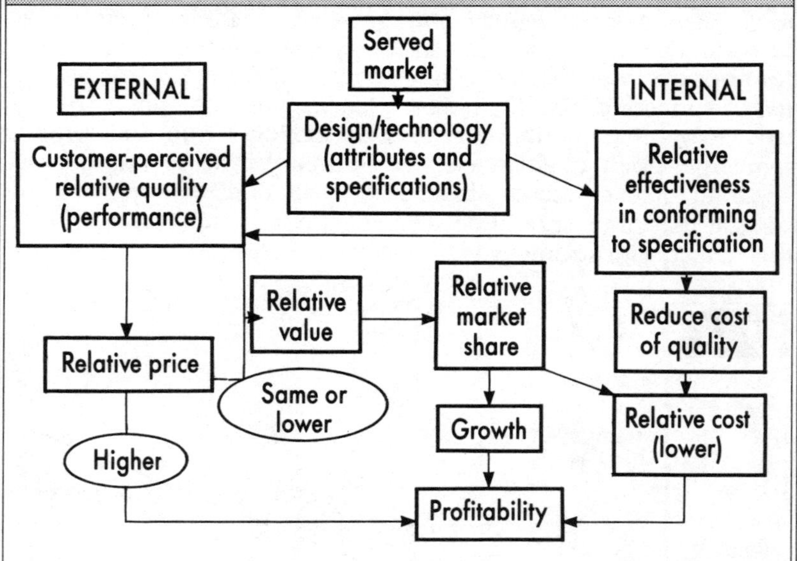

The effects of quality as a component of value both on contemporaneous profitability and future competitiveness that emerge from the PIMS data are extremely powerful and robust. It is surprising, therefore, that more serious attention has not been paid to such an apparently ubiquitous phenomenon. Until recently the PIMS results were known in detail only to experienced member-companies, and published material was sparse or in very summarised form. More extensive, multivariate studies have not been published, although they have been incorporated into the modelling procedures familiar to member-companies.

More probably, much of the neglect of quality as a major strategic issue is due to the vagueness of its meaning. It is not uncommon for the present writer to uncover several different meanings to the word 'quality' within any given management group. The tight definition specified by the original PIMS researchers is either never realised or easily lost in the operating cultures that equate quality with technical standards or conformity to specifications or engineering excellence. The importance of the customers' views and experience may not be appreciated, or even known. Also, *absolute* quality improvements may not mean *relative* quality improvements if competitors are raising their quality equally well.

A more frequent error is to see quality improvement as moving 'up-market' into some more glamorous niche. Not so: it is about doing better than competitors in whichever sector of the market you serve. Many companies that have a good reputation in the middle of the market may only be able to achieve poor relative standing in the upper end. For example, many Irish food products are perceived poorly in the UK (though not in Germany, where the same products are perceived as emanating from a pollution-free country). The best solution for poor quality is *to fix it*, not to escape the problem by attempting to go 'up-market'.

The power of relative quality can be seen even with product categories traditionally regarded as 'commodity', for example two elements of the national diet, bread and tea. The most significant consumer requirement in bread is 'freshness', which the purchaser tests by squeezing the product on the supermarket shelf. Those Irish bakeries that during the 1970s continued to bake at night to deliver this essential consumer requirement were rewarded with larger market shares.

Similarly those independent Irish tea companies, such as Barry's (others are mostly British-owned), who recognised the real and very critical taste requirements of the Irish tea drinker compared with the British consumer were rewarded with substantial market share gains and well-earned bargaining power with retail buyers.

Of course it is equally possible to indicate cases where price tactics clearly affected market share gains and losses, or where, as has often been expressed to the writer by business managers, 'I improved my quality and all I got was extra cost: there was no real effect on volume growth or market share.'

But it is too easy to jump to conclusions based on impressions or a single case. Business activity is a vital domain of modern society. Yet those who insist on the need for more methodical observation and analytical rigour are fighting a losing battle. In the case just mentioned, perhaps quality was being improved in an operating sense only but not in a customer-perceived sense. Or perhaps the change in quality had not yet registered on the customer's mind. A decision to upgrade quality is a strategic one. It takes time, and immediate costs in research and marketing often must be incurred. What the PIMS data show clearly is that once the improvement in relative quality has registered in the minds of customers, sustainable market share gains and falling relative costs are a usual result.

Other factors also are associated with the attainment of market share, such as, for example, increased marketing budgets. Increased expenditures on sales forces are particularly effective, thus lending support to those in Ireland who feel that 'worn shoe-leather' is a key to an improved trading position. New products were another key ingredient. Businesses in the PIMS data-base with high percentages of current sales (i.e. greater than 10 per cent) coming from recently introduced products showed marked gains in market share.

It is worth emphasising, however, that relative customer-perceived product quality was still the linchpin of competitive strategy in all market sectors, surpassing price, marketing, and innovation (new products). Putting marketing effort behind weak or inferior products is wasteful and counter-productive. New product launches are more expensive and hazardous for any business with a reputation for quality that has left much to be desired. If Ireland's reputation for quality in tourism, food and other products and services is poor or mediocre, the strategy priority is *to fix that problem*. The signs are that much has been and is being done in Ireland to improve and upgrade quality. It is gratifying to see how many companies are adopting 'total quality' and other programmes that aim at not only improving products but changing management cultures and employee attitudes towards a quality-conscious outlook. But much remains to be done. And even then it takes time for such improvements to take effect in a strategically significant sense.

GROWTH

How is what we have been saying related to growth? There are two ways in which Ireland can grow. It can be 'pulled' into growth by a reviving world economy (a rising tide raises all boats); or alternatively it can 'push' its own growth through the competitive strength of its corporate sector.

Ireland is too small to influence world growth. If it wishes for growth it must either wait for the rest of the world, or push growth through better competitive strategies. Since market share is tied very strongly to financial health, a gain in market share is a better form of growth. It represents a genuine acquisition of strength. Growth in output that comes from a reviving world economy can hide competitiveness weakness, but only until the next downturn. Competitiveness is a good bet either way (see fig. 5.7).

FIG 5.7

Employment growth (%)

Market share (% change per annum): −1, 4

Market volume growth (% change per annum): −1, 7

−7	−3	3
−2	2	8
5	8	19

Competitiveness creates jobs even in conditions of market decline. Lack of competitiveness destroys jobs even during modest growth.

Source: Carroll.[12]

We arranged the 3,000 PIMS businesses across rows according to falling shares and modest or strong gains in market shares, and down columns according to decline and modest or strong growth in market demand. The number in each cell represents the average annual growth in employment (over four years) among the businesses in each cell. The facts speak for themselves: competitive strength can create employment even in conditions of market decline; lack of competitive strength destroys jobs even in conditions of market growth.

CONCLUSION

Competitiveness matters. If Ireland wishes for growth and its resultant benefits, it has little choice but to develop a corporate sector with credible competitive strategies in international markets. The most important empirical evidence continues to show a strong relationship between financial health and market share. Competitiveness is at least about gaining 'adequate' market shares. Competitive strategy is multi-faceted, involving criteria for choice of attractive sectors together with the pursuit of the correct combination of factors to attain such an adequate market share. For Ireland, the most attractive sectors are more likely to be producer goods than consumer products. Quality-driven value is the only really credible means of attaining that end.

Notes

1. Bradley T. Gale and Robert D. Buzzell, 'Market Position and Competitive Strategy' (internal PIMS members' report), Boston (Mass.): Strategic Planning Institute 1987.
2. Imel Blake and Peter Helmherger, 'Estimation of the Structure-Profit Relationships with Application to the Food Processing Sector' in *American Economic Review*, September 1971, 614–27; Bradley T. Gale, 'Market Share and Rate of Return' in *Review of Economics and Statistics*, November 1972, 412–23; William G. Shephard, 'The Elements of Market Structure' in *Review of Economics and Statistics*, February 1972, 25–37.
3. David J. Ravenscraft, 'Structure-Profit Relationships at the Line of Business and Industry Level' in *Review of Economics and Statistics*, February 1983, 22–31.
4. Michael E. Porter, *Competitive Strategy Techniques for Analysing Industries and Competitors*, New York: Free Press 1980.
5. Boston Consulting Group, conference notes, 1981.
6. Charles Carroll, *Building Ireland's Business: Perspectives from PIMS*, Dublin: Irish Management Institute 1984.
7. Price Waterhouse (for the Department of Tourism and Transport), *Improving the Performance of Irish Tourism: Main Report*, Dublin: Stationery Office 1987.
8. Strategic Planning Institute, annual members' conferences, 1985 and 1986.
9. C. H. Murray, 'The Role of Exports in the Economy' in *Central Bank Review*, autumn 1981, 83–93.
10. Thomas J. Peters and Robert H. Wattermann, *In Search of Excellence: Lessons from America's Best-Run Companies*, Scranton (Pennsylvania): Harper and Row 1982.
11. Donald Clifford and Richard Cavanagh (eds.), *The Winning Performance: How America's High-Growth, Mid-Size Companies Succeed*, New York: Bantam 1985.
12. Charles Carroll, 'Business and Jobs: Evidence from PIMS' (Irish Management Institute seminar paper), January 1986.

COST COMPETITIVENESS AND HOW TO IMPROVE IT

Alan W. Gray

Indecon International Economic Consultants

Industrial competitiveness is a complex issue, and some of the important aspects of non-cost competitiveness are considered in subsequent chapters. Cost competitiveness is, however, partially under domestic control and has the potential to respond to appropriate action. While low costs are no substitute for improving other aspects of competitiveness, the harsh truth is that it is likely that the higher its unit costs in international currency, the smaller will be a country's share of world markets. This has obvious consequences for the sustainable level of output and employment.

In evaluating cost competitiveness and how to improve it, it is necessary to focus attention on those aspects of costs that are important and that are amenable to domestic influence. In chapter 3, details of the cost structure of Irish industry were presented. While the relative importance of particular cost items varies between sectors, industrial costs can be classified into the following four main areas: (*a*) labour costs; (*b*) imported raw material costs; (*c*) capital costs; and (*d*) domestic inputs. The cost of imported raw materials is largely outside domestic control, and as a result this chapter will focus most attention on the three other categories of costs.

6

LABOUR COSTS

Labour costs are one of the most important elements of domestic costs. On average, wages and salaries account for 40 per cent of net output, and for most firms they are the largest element of costs under domestic control. The level of labour costs directly impacts on the cost competitiveness of industrial enterprises and also influences the cost of services bought from other firms, and the cost of public services that are paid for by taxes. Developments in labour costs arise from a number of factors, including wages and salaries, non-wage labour costs, productivity, and exchange rates. All these factors have influenced the competitiveness of Irish industry.

In considering labour costs and industrial competitiveness, the cost to industry is determined by gross wages and salary costs, and also additional costs, of which PRSI and the costs of training and pensions are the most important. Non-pay labour costs also include the costs of absenteeism and work-days lost through industrial disputes. While the absolute level of costs is important, the vital issue is unit labour costs, which measure the labour cost of producing a unit of output. This takes into account the productivity of labour. Given the need for unit labour costs to remain competitive, it is only by increasing productivity that an increase in living standards could be secured.

This is not to suggest that the absolute level of labour costs is not important. There are two main reasons why absolute levels are of relevance. Firstly, an impetus to the establishment of foreign investment in Ireland is likely to be the absolute level of labour costs, as in many cases productivity is largely determined by the production process. It would, however, be a mistake to assume that the efficiency, skills and motivation of employees do not affect productivity. Secondly, if the absolute level of labour costs rises, firms may respond by substituting capital for labour, giving rise to what is known as capital-deepening, which is an increase in capital stock per employee. This may increase productivity and reduce unit labour costs, but will do so at lower levels of employment.

IMPORTED RAW MATERIALS

As indicated at the start of this chapter, the cost of imported raw materials is largely outside domestic control. The same conclusion applies to imported capital goods. The cost of imports will of course also be influenced by exchange rate developments (the important issue of exchange rate policy is considered in chapter 7). It should, however, be noted that there may be the potential to make some savings in these costs by efficiency in purchasing and stock control and by foreign exchange risk management. These issues are considered later in this chapter.

CAPITAL COSTS

The level of capital costs is an important aspect of competitiveness from the point of view of its impact on the level of investment, which in turn influences productivity and competitiveness. Capital costs are also of relevance in their contribution to overall costs. The cost of capital to firms in Ireland is influenced by interest and inflation rates, and also by taxation and industrial grants. Interest rates affect firms differently because of differences in taxation liabilities and also because of differences in debt/equity ratios. For firms that depend on equity capital, the cost of capital could be seen as the return on investment that is required to offer investors a high enough post-tax return to attract their funds.

The willingness of investors to provide equity capital is of course influenced by the taxation system, both in the tax treatment of alternative uses for their funds and the difference between the return on capital on their funds and the post-tax return that they receive, which is known as the 'tax wedge'.

COST OF DOMESTIC INPUTS

The cost of domestic inputs of goods and services refers to the bought-in requirements of industry from other enterprises and institutions in Ireland. This category of costs differs from imported raw materials in that these costs are to some extent under domestic control. The cost of these inputs is largely determined by the same elements of labour, capital and raw material costs as discussed previously. It is also useful to include taxation in this category, as this includes the costs to industry of public services. Domestic inputs include the cost of domestically produced raw materials and sub-supplies as well as the costs of utility services, such as electricity and communications. They also include a wide range of domestically supplied services. The increasing recourse of industrial firms to specialised service suppliers makes the cost of such services of growing importance.

POLICY RESPONSES

Having identified the main categories of domestically influenced industrial costs, it is important that we focus attention on what can be done to improve cost competitiveness. In this section we consider four approaches whereby governments have attempted to improve cost competitiveness, as follows: incomes and price control, macro-economic policies, competition policies, and industrial policies. We also consider what action can be taken directly by industry to improve its cost competitiveness.

Incomes and Price Control: Wages and price controls in various forms have in the past been used by governments in most western European countries as a policy response aimed at improving cost competitiveness. Given the dominant position for many firms of labour costs in cost competitiveness, it is understandable that attempts to control incomes should be considered. Price control is frequently used in association with an incomes policy in order to attempt to moderate inflation and thus minimise the impact on living standards of an incomes policy.

Most domestic costs constitute incomes, whether in the form of distributed profits, wages and salaries, or some other form of incomes. Income controls have been tried in a number of different forms, ranging from voluntary cost norms or recommendations to full statutory controls. Within this spectrum there are numerous options concerning the nature of an incomes policy, and a lot of fine tuning is feasible, at least in theory. Thus for example it is possible to have national wage agreements that cover features such as taxation and aspects of economic policy. It would also be possible to have a voluntary incomes policy but to ensure that the government did not assist any firms in which the pay norms had been exceeded: for example by restricting state grants and advisory services to firms with pay levels in accordance with income norms, or by making observance of a national pay norm a condition for obtaining government contracts.

The important question concerning both incomes and price controls is whether they are effective instruments in improving cost competitiveness. The effectiveness of an incomes policy can only be judged by the difference between what actually happened and what would otherwise have happened in the absence of any controls. Unfortunately it is possible to establish contradictory conclusions by *a priori* reasoning, and the results of empirical tests are often inconclusive. In evaluating incomes and price controls it is not sufficient to examine whether incomes and prices increased faster in periods of controls than when they were not operative, as controls are frequently introduced when inflation is accelerating. There are severe practical difficulties in attempting to measure whether incomes and price controls reduced the rate of change of wages (and prices) below what they otherwise would have been both during and after controls. Apart from the influence of underlying economic developments such as inflation, evaluating the impact of controls is made more difficult by the fact that the labour market may be affected by a change in some other government policy, such as monetary or fiscal policy.

There are many ways in which an incomes policy or price control might conceivably influence economic developments. They might for example restrict income growth to productivity growth, or might change the trade-off between unemployment and inflation. The impact of such different effects has important implications for the effectiveness of an incomes policy. It could be argued that while an incomes policy is unlikely to be effective on its own, it could be useful if accompanied by a monetary and fiscal policy that is consistent with a lower rate of wage and price changes. If policy makers attempt to maintain a disequilibrium position by means of controls, the result is likely to be an explosion in prices and incomes when controls are removed.

It should be realised that even if an incomes and price control policy reduced the inflation rate, it is necessary to weigh up the costs of such policies in administration costs and market distortions. If controls are more than pay norms, they may have the drawback of needing significant administration, which can be inflexible. The costs of incomes and price controls, even if effective, have to take account of the fact that they distort the allocation of labour and capital between different uses by restricting movements in incomes and prices. This problem is of some significance when a faster than average wage increase in some sectors may be an indication of improving overall competitiveness and the need to attract additional resources to service the market sector involved. A further potential problem with price control is that if prices are set below the equilibrium price there will be unfulfilled demand. Of greater concern is the fact that some commentators believe that both the variance and the acceleration of inflation have been aggravated by government intervention in incomes and price determination.

The problems with income policies have led some economists to argue that market forces should determine pay and price developments. It is, however, useful to consider the issue of incomes and price control policies for three different categories of economic activity: for firms facing international competition, for firms in the non-traded sector, and for the non-market public sector. For firms that have to compete with international competition there will be market pressures to remain cost-competitive. For firms that fail to respond to such pressures, lost market share and ultimately closure are the likely outcome. For such firms, government-imposed price control does not make sense, and an incomes policy that reduces the firm's flexibility is likely to be inappropriate. While an incomes or pay norm might be useful in altering expectations, the argument for any type of incomes policy for such firms is weaker than for the public sector or for firms in the non-traded sector.

For firms in the non-traded (or protected/sheltered) sector (which is defined as firms that are not exposed to international competition, for example some suppliers of local services or raw materials or utilities), the case for incomes and price control is stronger. This would take account of the impact of non-competitive market conditions in the non-traded sector, which could enable firms to increase incomes faster than productivity growth and, because of their market power, to pass on these increases in higher prices to firms that have to meet international competition. Enterprises in Ireland that are competing with overseas suppliers are in general not in a position to dictate price increases, and if input costs from the non-traded sector increase, this is likely to result in declining output and employment. Because of their impact on the internationally traded sector, incomes and price controls are frequently applied to the non-traded sector. If, however, the cause of the problem in the non-traded sector is lack of competition, the best policy response would be to attempt to deal directly with this issue, as this is likely to minimise any distortions in resource allocation. This may not, of course, be feasible in all cases, but the potential for using competition policies to tackle uncompetitive pricing in the non-traded sector is an important potential policy response, which is considered later in this chapter.

For the public sector, incomes policy can be used to attempt to alter the trade-off between incomes and employment that arises when there are budgetary limitations on public expenditure. It is, however, important to ensure that unjustified gaps do not emerge between public and private sector incomes that result in a 'brain drain' from the public sector.

Fiscal and Monetary Policies: Cost competitiveness is influenced by the environment in which industry operates, which in turn is in part determined by government macroeconomic policies. It is therefore useful to consider the impact on the cost competitiveness of some aspects of macroeconomic policies. In particular it is useful to focus on the impact of developments in public finances, in taxation, and in exchange controls.

One of the main determinants of capital costs is the development of interest and inflation rates. While the determinants of interest and inflation are uncertain, it is clear that they are influenced by government policy in relation to public finances. While Irish interest rates are largely determined by international developments, a failure to correct the imbalance in the Irish public finances would put an upward pressure on interest rates through its impact in creating uncertainty regarding the exchange rate and by exerting pressure on domestic money markets.

The Government's taxation policies directly impact on cost competitiveness by influencing the cost of labour, capital, and domestic inputs. While the cost of labour to industry is, as outlined earlier, determined by pay and non-pay costs, the employee is primarily concerned with after-tax pay levels. The level of personal tax and social security taxes is therefore a direct influence on the level of labour costs. The taxation of different types of investments also affects the relative attractiveness of investments in industry, which as a consequence influences the costs of capital. While there have been some important taxation adjustments in recent years to take account of this factor, there is still likely to be scope for modifying the tax system to favour after-tax returns of investment in the internationally traded sector.

Providing greater access for Irish firms to the stock market, which is a major source of corporate financing in other industrialised countries, is also likely to assist industrial competitiveness.

Competition Policies: Firms operating in competitive markets have no option but to remain competitive if they are to survive and expand. In a competitive market, producers will look for ways to reduce costs, usually by making the production process more efficient. Competition encourages the efficient allocation of resources and stimulates firms to better their performance relative to their competitors. In such a situation incomes and prices are 'controlled' by market conditions. In these circumstances firms that are not cost-competitive are driven out of business. Even in such competitive markets, incomes can rise to levels that create unemployment as firms respond to increasing real wage costs by substituting capital for labour. In these circumstances governments may wish to alter the trade-off between capital and labour by fiscal and industrial policies.

Where firms are not exposed to international competition, an appropriate policy response that can be used to improve cost competitiveness is for governments to take steps to increase competition. This can be achieved by policies aimed at the removal of restrictive practices and other forms of collusive market behaviour, and by introducing restrictions on certain types of mergers. Policies that result in deregulation can also have a dramatic impact on competition and on prices. The problem for a country like Ireland is that in many cases the non-traded market may not be sufficient, because of economies of scale, to support a competitive productive structure. Thus the potential to use anti-trust policies is likely to be much less in Ireland than in the large industrial countries, such as the United States, where they are a key policy instrument in encouraging competition. There is likely, however, to be much greater potential for policy initiatives in Ireland that would remove restrictive practices and encourage a more competitive market, particularly in those areas of the sheltered sector that supply internationally traded industry. Ireland should also actively remove any non-tariff barriers to trade that may at present be protecting manufacturing or service industries, and should demand similar action by other European Community countries.

Industrial Policies: In Ireland there is an extensive and complicated set of industrial policies in operation that have directly affected industrial cost competitiveness. In particular there are significant fiscal and grant incentives for investments in fixed capital and in activities such as product development and marketing. It is likely that these incentives are particularly attractive for new start-up investments, while the benefits are reduced for firms that have been operating for some time. Recent changes in industrial policy have attempted to take account of this point, but it is nevertheless likely to be a focus of increased debate.

A survey of industry in Ireland, however, indicated that taxation was identified as the main method by which the Government could assist industry, followed by lower costs for public utilities. Grants and subsidies ranked as much less important. This may reflect the current high level of incentives; and 51 per cent of respondents indicated that combined cuts in spending on industry and income tax reductions would not be good for business, while 49 per cent felt this would be desirable.[1] Some economists believe that continued Government assistance may give wrong signals as to the need to be competitive, and makes it easier for firms to sustain uncompetitive costs. It is clear that increased attention will have to be paid to evaluating the cost effectiveness of industrial policy and to looking directly at the causes of cost competitiveness.

In addition to industrial policies there are a range of other microeconomic policies, including energy and transport policies, that impact on industrial costs. The cost of such items as energy, transport and telecommunications is likely to be in part determined by Government policies on taxation, competition, and incomes and price control, which were discussed earlier.

Action by Industry: In considering what can be done to improve cost competitiveness it is important not to overlook the potential for action by industry. Significant improvements in cost competitiveness have been achieved by some firms, from changes in industrial logistics and in purchasing strategy. The potential for cost reductions by introducing technology—through its wide-ranging contribution to an increased productivity potential in all factors of production, from labour, capital, materials and energy to inventory stock control—is noteworthy. A cost leadership strategy can also be secured by improving flexibility and motivation and reducing absenteeism. This of course is a difficult challenge for all involved in industry, but might in some cases be assisted by the introduction of profit-sharing arrangements. It is noteworthy for example that in many cases the annual bonus in Japan is equal to wage costs.

Capital costs for industry could also be reduced by an increasing willingness to accept outside investors. Changes in the debt-equity ratio of firms could make a sizeable difference on the impact of interest rate changes. The costs of imported raw materials and imported capital equipment could be reduced by more effective exchange rate management. Most small and medium-sized firms do not consider the need to manage their foreign exchange position, and there is significant potential for reducing costs by using the newer products, such as options and the hedge market, and the instruments that are now available to manage interest rate exposures. Even very small percentage cost reductions in these areas could be significant.

CONCLUSIONS

It is critical for industry in Ireland to expand if progress is to be made on the two key problems of public finances and unemployment. While non-cost items are of central importance, it is also essential that Ireland maintains a cost leadership position. If cost competitiveness is not achieved, the potential for increasing market share and output will be damaged. In considering how to improve cost competitiveness, attention must focus on those costs that are under domestic influence.

The analysis in this chapter indicated that while incomes and price controls have been extensively used they are not likely to represent the best policy option and are probably inappropriate for enterprises exposed to international competition. For firms in the sheltered sector the case for incomes and prices control may be stronger. On balance, my view is that we probably should consider controls only where it is not possible to encourage competitive prices by removing restrictive practices and monopolistic market structures.

There is in my opinion, therefore, likely to be significant scope for policy initiatives aimed at encouraging market competition.

Where a competitive market cannot be secured, an incomes policy may be appropriate, but such initiatives should incorporate maximum flexibility. Where price control is introduced, for example where monopoly public utilities are concerned, the focus should be on an attempt to set prices at competitive levels and not on a cost-plus basis. In practice such calculations are likely to be difficult, but it is important that some equitable objectives are set in relation to utility prices. This also has implications for Government-imposed non-commercial practices. It is essential that such practices are paid for directly through taxation.

In the public sector there is, by definition, likely to be an incomes policy, and the key issue relates to the level at which incomes are agreed and what other economic policy issues are included in any such agreement. If pay in the public sector increases faster than productivity, the higher resultant costs imposed through taxation are likely to result in job losses elsewhere in the economy. Pay levels in the public sector must not, however, be restricted to levels that result in loss of the most able senior personnel. For the internationally traded sector, a pay norm recommendation, in contrast to a formal incomes policy, is more justifiable and could serve a useful role in highlighting the implications for employment of income increases that are not justified by output growth.

In formulating a response to cost competitiveness, the impact of developments in public finances, and in taxation, should be given priority. In particular it is important that the adjustment to the public finances continues. It is also important that tax reform be introduced to remove the negative impact of taxation on competitiveness.

Industrial policy should focus on developing competitive industry and not attempt to compensate through subsidies for uncompetitive cost structures. Finally, it is important not to overlook the potential for improving competitiveness by action taken within industrial enterprises. With a concerted action programme by Government, utilities, and industry, it is possible to develop a cost leadership position for industry in Ireland that would provide the basis for economic recovery.

Notes

1. Department of Industry and Commerce, *Review of Industrial Performance, 1986,* Dublin: Stationery Office (Pl. 4769) 1987.

EXCHANGE RATE POLICY AND COMPETITIVENESS

Brendan M. Walsh

University College, Dublin

An index of competitiveness measures the trend over time of a country's prices and costs relative to those of its trading partners, all expressed in a common currency. If this is rising, cost competitiveness is deteriorating.

Fig. 7.1 shows the trend in Irish competitiveness by comparing Irish labour costs relative to the EEC and Britain, and the overall average, since 1978. It may be seen that there was a deterioration of about 20 per cent in Irish overall competitiveness over the period 1978–86 according to this index. This has potentially serious implications for the ability of Irish firms to compete successfully on foreign and domestic markets, and consequently for the level of employment and unemployment in this country.

FIG. 7.1 **Measures of Competitiveness: Trend in Relative Wage Rates in a Common Currency, 1978–87**

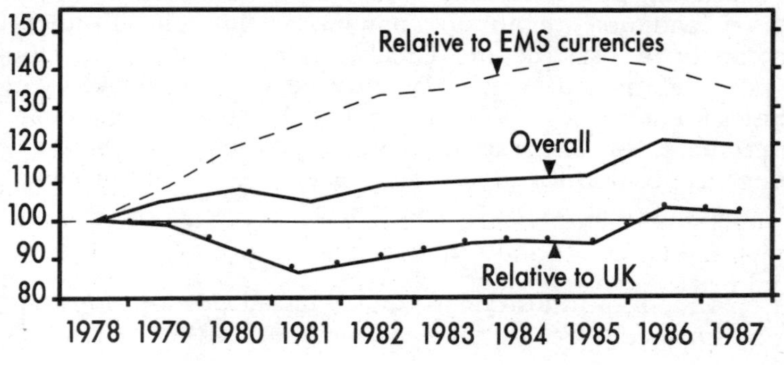

Source: OECD

In this chapter the role of exchange rate policy in relation to the trend of competitiveness is examined. The limited space available precludes discussing in any detail the interaction between movements in the exchange rate and movements in domestic costs, or exploring the magnitude of the impact of changes in competitiveness on the level of economic activity in Ireland. (This topic is dealt with in chapter 4.)

THE INTERNATIONAL SETTING

Since the early 1970s the rates of exchange between the major currencies of the western world have fluctuated widely. Despite repeated attempts by the governments and central banks of the main countries to restore stability, the amplitude of these fluctuations increased during the 1980s. Exchange rate volatility and the accompanying risk of misalignments continue to preoccupy policy-makers.

That fluctuating exchange rates can significantly alter international relative prices and costs in a very short period can be readily illustrated by considering the recent movements of the Irish pound/US dollar exchange rate. In March 1985 the Irish pound was worth 92 cents. By the end of 1987 it had risen to $1.66, an increase of 80 per cent. During this 20-month period the difference between the rates of cost and price inflation in the two countries was relatively slight, so that the change in the *nominal* rate of exchange was almost fully reflected in the *real* rate. The implications for the pattern of international trade and investment of such major changes in countries' relative costs and prices are enormous.

Ireland does not influence the exchange rate policies of the major economic powers. While as members of the European Communities we had some input into the proposals that led to the creation of the European Monetary System (EMS) in 1979, we have not been able to alter the UK's decision to remain outside the exchange rate fixing mechanism, which is the most important feature of the system.

Until 1979 the Irish authorities did not exercise an active exchange rate policy. In the years after independence the most important tasks were seen as ensuring the soundness and international acceptability of the currency, and facilitating international payments for importers and exporters. Preserving the link with sterling seemed to be the best way of achieving these objectives, in view of the importance of that currency in world finance and the fact that almost all our external trade was with the sterling area. The declining status of sterling as an international currency, its repeated devaluation against the US dollar and the growing diversification of Irish trade prompted some discussion of alternatives to the sterling link, but no change was seriously contemplated. Membership of the European Communities in the 1970s and sterling's rapid exit from the precursor of the EMS (the 'Snake') provoked a more extended discussion of the possibility of breaking the link, especially in the light of the important implications of exchange rate movements for the value of our receipts from the Common Agricultural Policy. But despite the changed environment, the link with sterling was retained, because no realistic alternative was available.

The agreement to form the EMS in 1978 radically changed the context of Irish exchange rate policy. We were offered the prospect of joining a new grouping of currencies which, if sterling were included, would ensure exchange rate stability with the countries that account for over two-thirds of our trade. By joining we would continue to play the role of 'good Europeans' and, as a bonus, we would share with Italy in a significant subsidy to offset the deflationary bias inherent in trying to stabilise our exchange rate through a basket of currencies in which the German mark has the largest weight. The new alignment would also mean that Ireland would no longer automatically import Britain's high rate of inflation.

FIG. 7.2 **Sterling Exchange Rate Quarterly averages**

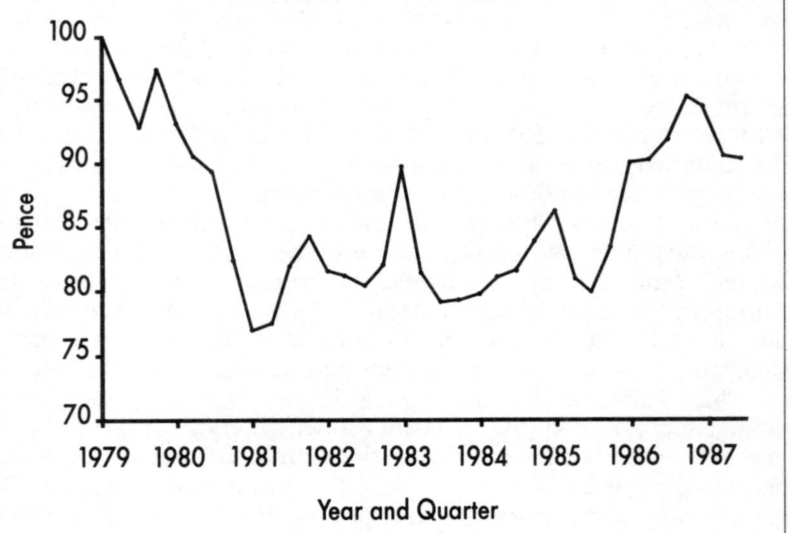

In the event, Britain decided not to participate in the exchange rate peg that is the most important feature of the EMS, and we decided to join anyway. Initially there was the possibility that sterling would remain stable relative to EMS currencies, so that we could honour our commitment to the system without breaking with sterling. However, the unexpected surge of sterling on the foreign exchange markets at the end of March 1979 made this impossible, and the sterling link was broken. The Irish pound has fluctuated relative to sterling for the last nine years (fig. 7.2).

THE IRISH POUND IN THE EMS

Our exchange rate policy since 1979 has been dominated by our obligations under the EMS. Formally these comprise the setting of 'central rates' against the six other currencies in the system, and co-operating to ensure that the value of the Irish pound does not rise above or fall below the point at which the spread between the strongest and weakest currencies in the grid exceeds 2.25 per cent around these rates. (The Italian lira is allowed a 6 per cent spread, but we decided against any concession of this nature.) This obligation has been discharged quite smoothly. The Central Bank intervenes on the foreign exchanges when necessary to support or sell the Irish pound to prevent it exceeding its limits in the EMS, but does not release information on the amount spent on intervention.

FIG. 7.3

Exchange Rate in EMS
Quarterly averages, weighted against narrow-band EMS currencies

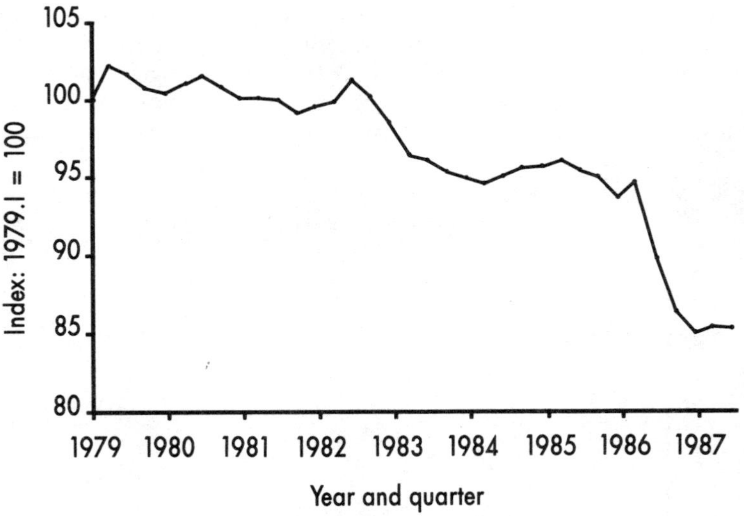

We participate in the discussions surrounding the realignments that have been a regular feature of the operation of the system. In the early years of membership we tended to 'go through the middle' between German revaluations and French and Italian devaluations with the result that the average value of the Irish pound was almost stable within the system between 1979 and the end of 1982 (fig. 7.3). However, in March 1983 and again in August 1986 we devalued (by 8.5 per cent against the German mark and Dutch guilder on the first occasion, and by 8 per cent against all the EMS currencies on the second). Over the entire period of membership, the average value of the Irish pound has fallen by about 15 per cent, or 1.5 per cent a year, against the currencies in the 'narrow band' exchange rate peg, with larger depreciations occurring relative to the German mark and the

Dutch guilder. In this sense we have operated an 'adjustable peg' within the EMS. However, the decline of the Irish pound has been relatively smooth, and volatility has been kept to a minimum. This is in marked contrast with the wide swings that have occurred in the Irish pound/sterling exchange rate.

THE EFFECTIVE EXCHANGE RATE

In 1986 the EMS accounted for just under 50 per cent of our total exports and 35 per cent of our imports. These proportions are small compared with the importance of intra-EMS trade for all the other members. The continued absence of our largest trading partner, the UK, from the exchange rate peg is a major drawback to membership from the Irish perspective. This became very clear in 1983 when sterling's decline relative to the currencies of the EMS caused the Irish pound to rise to 87p sterling, leading to a serious loss of competitiveness relative to British firms. To redress this difficulty the Irish pound was devalued at the March realignment. History repeated itself in August 1986 when the renewed weakness of sterling threatened to push the Irish pound back to 1:1 parity. On this occasion we devalued without a general EMS realignment.

FIG. 7.4 **Effective Exchange Rate Index**
Quarterly averages

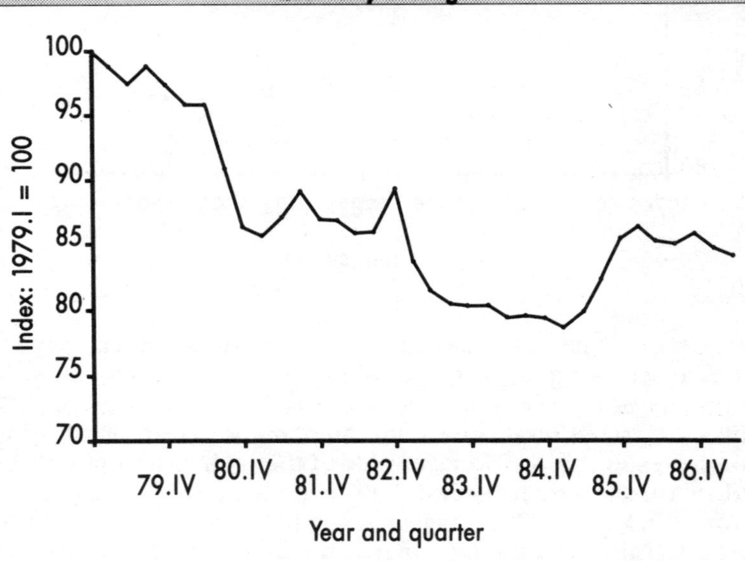

To obtain a comprehensive picture of the external value of the Irish pound it is necessary to look at an index of its value against a basket of currencies that includes sterling and the US dollar as well as the EMS currencies. The Central Bank publishes an effective exchange

FIG 7.5 Exchange Rate Indices Quarterly averages

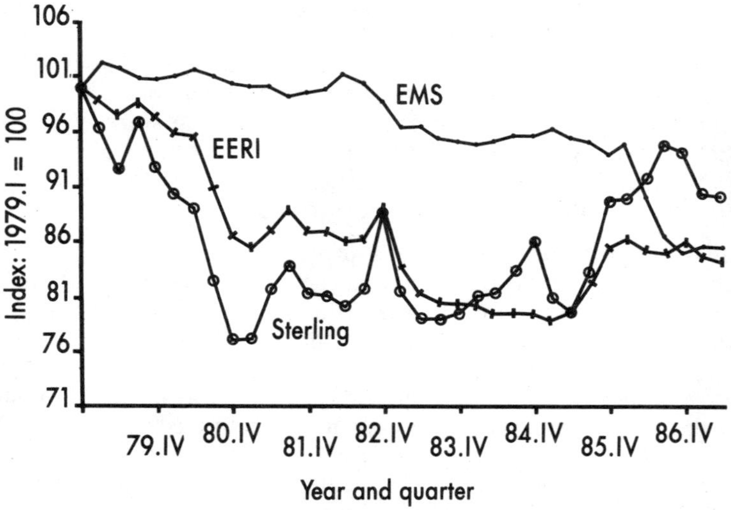

rate index (EERI), based on an unpublished set of weights, which averages the value of the Irish pound with the currencies of our main trading partners. Fig. 7.4 shows how this index has behaved since 1978. The destabilising effect on the EERI of the volatility of sterling relative to the EMS currencies is evident from fig. 7.5, where the sterling and EMS rates are shown on the same scale as the EERI.

During 1979 and 1980 the sharp decline in the EERI reflected the decline of the Irish pound against sterling. The further decline in 1983 was due to the devaluation within the EMS and the continued fall relative to the dollar. After a period of stability from the end of 1983 to mid-1985, the Irish pound began to rise against the EMS currencies, sterling, and the dollar, with the result that the EERI rose by over 10 per cent between June 1985 and March 1986. Relative to sterling the Irish pound rose by about 20 per cent. The August devaluation had the effect of stabilising the EERI at about 85 per cent of its 1979 value, despite the further weakness of sterling later in the year. It required the sharp appreciation of sterling that occurred in 1987 to lower the EERI to a more sustainable level.

REAL EXCHANGE RATES

From the point of view of competitiveness, it is real or inflation-adjusted exchange rates that matter. For example, the value of the Irish pound relative to the German mark has fallen by 30 per cent since 1979, but Irish labour costs have risen by more than 30 per cent in excess of the rise in German labour costs over this period. Thus, in real terms our exchange rate has risen relative to Germany, because the fall in the nominal rate has not been sufficient to fully offset the differential between Irish and German rates of wage inflation.

Fig 7.1 displayed the nominal exchange rates relative to the EMS, Britain, and an overall average, adjusted by the rates of change in wages in manufacturing industry over the years 1979–86. According to this measure of the real exchange rate there has been an overall decline of about 20 per cent in Irish competitiveness since we joined the EMS. This has occurred because the 40 per cent loss of competitiveness relative to the EMS countries has not been offset by a competitive gain relative to sterling or the US dollar.

It is beyond the scope of this short chapter to evaluate in any depth what effect these trends in real exchange rates have had on the economy. It may be noted that despite the major loss of competitiveness relative to the EMS countries since 1978, both the absolute volume and the relative importance of our exports to them have grown significantly. The rapid growth in Irish exports seems to have occurred for reasons that have little to do with Irish cost competitiveness. Most of these exports are from subsidiaries of foreign firms in the pharmaceutical, electrical engineering and instrument engineering sectors, which are not sensitive to local labour costs. Tax planning has played an important role in their decision to locate in Ireland, and a substantial proportion of the profits arising from their exports is repatriated. On the other hand, more employment-intensive industrial sectors and tourism are likely to have been adversely affected by the deteriorating trend in relative costs during the 1980s.

During the period 1979–82 we enjoyed a significant competitive gain relative to Britain, due to the dramatic real appreciation of sterling. However, after 1982 sterling weakened significantly on the foreign exchanges, with the result that by 1986 all of this competitive gain had been lost (fig. 7.1). The more traditional industrial sectors that rely heavily on the British market tended to contract over this entire period, but this trend was most pronounced early in 1983 and during most of 1986, when the weakness of sterling caused severe competitive problems for many firms. They enjoyed a respite as sterling strengthened in 1987.

EXCHANGE RATE POLICY

Since joining the EMS, our exchange rate policy has been based on maintaining the average value of our currency within the system. While this objective has been modified to avert sudden increases in the overall value of the currency, it has from time to time entailed a significant loss of competitiveness, because we have not devalued sufficiently to offset the full inflation differential between us and the average of our trading partners.

The rationale for this 'non-accommodating' exchange rate policy has been the expectation that it would bestow important net benefits on our economy. By making it difficult for employers to concede unwarranted wage claims, and by moderating the rate of imported inflation, the policy was expected to place the economy in a virtuous circle in which the rate of inflation would spiral downwards. This would replace the vicious circle of currency depreciation and rising costs and prices into which we were locked during the 1970s. In the pre-EMS discussions there was widespread optimism that the 'hard currency peg' to which we believed we were committing ourselves would lead to convergence of our inflation and interest rates to German levels, within months rather than years.

For most of the ten years that we have been members of the EMS the outcome has been at variance with these expectations. In the first place, we did not maintain our nominal exchange rate rigidly fixed relative to the hard currencies of the system. Instead we pursued a policy of allowing some of our higher rate of inflation to be offset through periodic devaluations. However, we did not operate an outright 'crawling peg', inasmuch as the fall in our exchange rate did not fully accommodate the differential between our rate of inflation and that of Germany. The resultant loss of competitiveness did not, however, appear to exercise a marked moderating influence on our rate of inflation, and a large gap between Irish and German rates of interest persisted. In fact it was not until 1988 that Ireland could

FIG. 7.6 **The EMS and the Irish Pound/Sterling Rate**

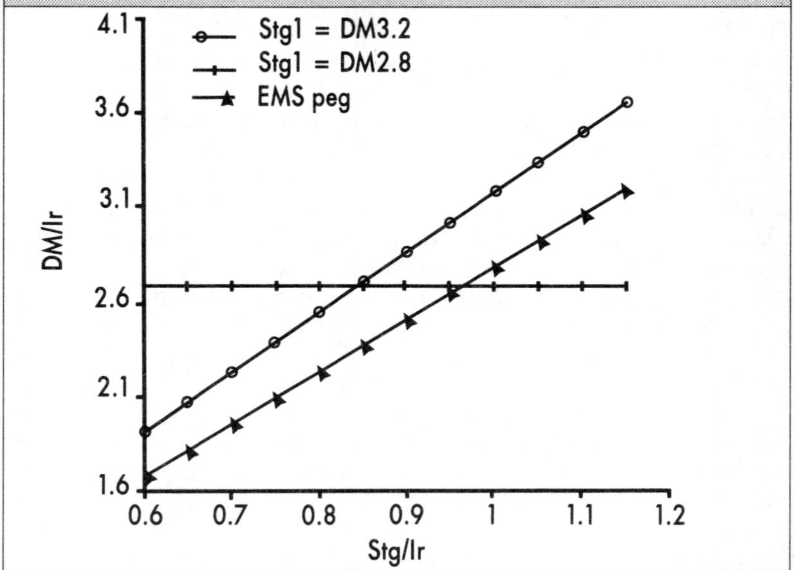

clearly be seen to enjoy the expected benefits of membership of the EMS, as our rates of inflation and interest moved significantly below British levels. The changed stance of fiscal policy, rather than any change in our exchange rate policy, was mainly responsible for these favourable developments.

A contradiction between these two statements of policy could arise from the movement of the pound sterling relative to the EMS and the impact of this on our EERI, as in 1983 and 1986. There are only two independent exchange rates between sterling (Stg), the Irish pound (Ir), and the German mark (DM). Given the value of the Ir/DM rate, to which we are pegged within the EMS, the Ir/Stg rate follows arithmetically from the Stg/DM rate, over which we have no control. The problem of reconciling targets both for sterling and the EMS (represented by the DM) is illustrated in fig. 7.6. The diagram shows how a given EMS central rate could become incompatible with a desired Stg/Ir rate due to a shift in the Stg/DM rate. In view of the volatility exhibited by sterling relative to the DM in the past, it is clear that the 2.25 per cent band around the central Ir/DM rate affords very little protection from a misaligned Ir/Stg rate.

The second dilemma facing Irish policy-makers concerns the broad issue of the costs and benefits of a 'hard currency peg'. Despite our non-accommodating exchange rate policies, the expected convergence of our rates of interest and inflation to German levels did not occur for most of the 1980s. Moreover, the tenuousness of the benefits of the EMS link was illustrated during the last quarter of 1986 when difficulties in funding the exchequer borrowing requirement led to a sudden loss of confidence in our currency and a sharp widening of the Irish/EMS interest differential in the absence of supporting fiscal and monetary policies. Similarly, the favourable developments that were evident in the Irish economy during 1988 are more readily accounted for by fiscal than exchange rate policy.

A conscious policy of devaluation to stimulate the level of output and employment seems to have been ruled out by the Irish authorities. In the words of the OECD survey, they believe that 'empirical studies show that . . . the only lasting effect tends to be on inflation with no permanent impact on the real economy.'[1] They may also believe that the economy has now adjusted to the prevailing level of exchange rates and that a devaluation would not restore any of the output and employment lost as a result of the real appreciation of earlier years: when firms go out of business due to a loss of competitiveness, the labour force is dispersed, plant is dismantled, and markets may be lost for ever. If this is the case, a fall in the exchange rate is unlikely to reverse this train of events. This line of argument highlights how important it is to avoid a loss of competitiveness in the first place.

The influence of the exchange rate on the rate of inflation during the 1980s is not obvious from the record. The decline in the value of the currency early in the decade did not lead to an acceleration in Irish inflation relative to British, whilst its rise during 1986 seemed to have equally little impact on relative rates of inflation. Estimates of the likely effect of a devaluation in present circumstances should allow for the impact of the exceptionally depressed labour market and how this may alter the response to a devaluation compared with what happened during the 1970s.

The poor performance of the Irish economy relative to the EEC as a whole since we joined the EMS gives no grounds for confidence that the exchange rate policy we have pursued over these years has been that most appropriate for our circumstances. The relatively favourable experiences of Sweden and Belgium following substantial devaluations in the 1980s show that exchange rate adjustment, in tandem with incomes and budgetary policies, can make a contribution to the correction of macroeconomic imbalances in small open economies. It is also relevant to note the contribution of the decline in sterling during 1986 to the rapid growth of the British economy during 1987. Some of the recent improvement in the Irish economy must be attributed to the fall in our exchange rate during 1987/88.

CONCLUSION

The exchange rate policy we have pursued since 1979 has been based on the belief that domestic costs would be brought under control by not devaluing sufficiently to accommodate our relatively high rate of inflation. We have enjoyed some benefits from this policy, but we have paid a price in deteriorating competitiveness, which may have contributed to the economic decline that has been experienced during the 1980s, the most serious manifestations of which are the sharp fall in employment and the crisis levels of unemployment and emigration. It is my view that in the future, exchange rate policy should place more emphasis on maintaining competitiveness than was done during the 1980s. This would require a greater readiness to devalue to avert a real appreciation of the Irish pound and the resultant loss of competitiveness.

Notes

1. Organisation for Economic Co-operation and Development, *Economic Survey of Ireland, 1987/88,* Paris: OECD 1987, 76.

INNOVATION: NEW PROPERTY RIGHTS ARE BETTER THAN STATE INVOLVEMENT

William Kingston

Trinity College, Dublin

Does more research and development (R&D) lead to a more competitive economy? By no means necessarily. The UK is close to the top of the R&D/GDP ratio league, yet it has a negative (and worsening) balance of trade in manufactures. The relationship between R&D and competitive products is complex, non-linear in effect, uncertain in the direction of causality, and every bit as weak as that between capital formation and economic growth.

In the late 1970s, for example, Irish investment in machinery and equipment as a proportion of GDP was significantly higher than Japan's, yet the returns on this investment during the 1980s for the two countries could hardly have differed more.[1] There is no reason to think that Irish spending on R&D has done any better. Interested parties regularly call attention to Ireland's relatively low rate of R&D spending by international standards, and demand that it should be increased. But in fact it is *too high* for the development of a competitive economy, because so much of it is controlled by bureaucrats in the employ of the state: the Japanese record alone is overwhelming evidence that for the development of competitive products, 'it is commercially funded and oriented R&D that correlates with commercial results.'[2]

8

This Irish R&D expenditure pattern is merely one aspect of national credulity about the value of state intervention in the economy, or industrial policy. Three successive and overlapping waves of cash flows from abroad both fostered intervention and postponed the growth of awareness that it does not work. Ireland in fact is a perfect example of how intervention results in an economically derivative society, characterised above all by inability to innovate. Dawning recognition of this during the last Government's term is reflected in the OECD's study of innovation policy in Ireland.[3] But this, being largely dependent, as these supranational documents are, on tendentious material supplied by local civil servants, proposes as a solution a series of initiatives that are bound to fail. This is inevitable, because the report relies on continuing intervention to bring about the hoped-for results. It blames current difficulties on the fact that earlier interventionist policies were 'not sufficiently directed towards supporting innovation', not on the *very existence* of such policies. Its recommendations leave all the state agencies and apparatus in place (even calling for more power and responsibility for some of them[4]), when what is needed is to replace them with new kinds of individual property rights that would enable creative energy to flourish in the economic field through decentralised decision-making.

MARKET FAILURE THEORY

Public financial support of R&D everywhere is the result of alliances between politicians who think there is a simple linear relationship between it and products that will produce money and jobs, bureaucrats who want power without personal responsibility, and academic scientists who simply want more money for research. Its record is one of consistent failure, which has often been spectacular.[5] It does *not* lead to competitive products, nor to economic growth through innovation.[6] Spending public money on science only tends to produce more science, not competitive products. And, where their effectiveness has been measured, subsidies to firms for R&D have not been justified by results.[7]

The case for intervention rests on the premise that, left to itself, private enterprise will not do the 'right' things, or enough of them. This is because market forces direct private-sector activity to areas of lowest risk and quickest profit. Because of its high risks and long timescale, innovation is held to be a classic case of such 'market failure', requiring that the state step in to fill the gap.

This view, however, ignores the truth that real-world markets are not part of the structure of the universe, but are social artefacts. They are structures of positive law, especially in relation to property rights.[8] Much market failure, therefore, is in fact *legal* failure. Developing new kinds of law to generate an environment within which individuals acting freely in their own interest also serve the common good is always an alternative to intervention. It is one moreover with an unmatched record of success, since it is the evolution of property rights, more recently in relation to information, that has been primarily responsible for the innovation on which the world's wealth is based.[9]

This is not to claim that everything can be left to decentralised decisions. But they have far more potential than they are being allowed to realise, because all three parties in the alliance that favours public support for R&D invariably raise the cry of 'market failure' too soon. They perceive, correctly, that the alternative—creative law-making—is arduous, gives no scope for empire-building, and produces less money for fundamental research.

THE LINEAR VIEW OF INNOVATION

Because invention comes before innovation in time, it is often simplistically assumed that there is a linear progression from basic research to applied research to product development to products that can compete in the market. In fact, whether products are competitive or not is primarily a function of their market power, and scientific R&D may be no more than one component in one type of market power. Further, any linearity there is in the process of developing new products may often run *backwards,* i.e. from market intelligence to development to applied research and (very rarely and very modestly) to basic research. Spending public money at the R&D end in the hope of finding a fairy godmother at the market end (as the Irish state is currently doing through its new NBST-IIRS hybrid 'Eolas') is precisely the kind of public-sector fantasy that has led the country into a mire of debt.

However, the harm of having bureaucrats in charge of funding R&D is by no means limited to the cases where they are actually responsible for carrying out the research. It is also apparent when they administer grants to assist private firms to carry out R&D. Innovators and bureaucrats do not have mutual imaginative rapport (to put it mildly), so the firms that get grants inevitably tend to be those whose managements are most like the grant-givers. When intervention reaches the stage of replacing law to a substantial extent, as in the Irish case, it generates a dependent management class, incapable of innovation or of developing competitive products, irrespective of the amount of public money thrown at it. This has even begun to be recognised in Ireland, as what is called the 'grant mentality', but it has yet to be widely understood that it is an inescapable consequence of using intervention instead of law to achieve economic aims.

Belief in market failure is probably the deepest of all elements in the Irish view of industry and economics. Every revolution is partly against prevailing property rights. Since the British system had contributed so much of the law that makes innovation possible, it was probably inevitable that, in reaction, the Irish should opt for a more collectivist approach. But there have been other factors. Politicians who are selected by multi-seat proportional representation are the least able of all to resist lobbies for intervention.[10] Irish senior public-sector employees tend not to have family backgrounds in industry. The influence of Keynes, mediated by academic economists who, like their scientific colleagues, have been only too ready to tap a new and rich source of funding, has provided intellectual justification for policies that expanded the role of the state.[11] The Irish public sector is consequently particularly antagonistic to any development that would use law to enable decentralised decisions, about R&D or anything else, to be taken by business people on their own.

THE BES AND HYSTER CASES

Tax relief on equity investment in private firms (the Business Expansion Scheme) is a case in point. The ideas on which the British government acted were available simultaneously to the Irish one, but were ignored.[12] The minister who eventually wished to follow British success with them met intense civil service opposition, so that the Irish copy is hedged around with restrictions, some of which are altogether absurd. For example, the relief was explicitly intended to take the place of state grants.[13] But in service industries it is only obtainable *in association with an IDA grant,* and this grant cannot be just for a feasibility study.[14] An incentive specifically intended to get investors to risk their money, therefore, is not available to them when the risk is highest, but only if and when it is lowered!

What happened in the case of Hyster is perhaps even more revealing. An Irish judicial decision followed British precedent in extending copyright protection to functional objects. According to this, copying a three-dimensional object infringes the artistic copyright in the drawings from which it has been made.[15] The resulting new type of protection showed itself to be extremely valuable for the types of innovation most suited to smaller firms. This was recognised in Britain, to the extent of establishing a new 'unregistered design right' by statute.[16] In Ireland, however, Hyster, a multinational favourite of the IDA, proposed to take over the former Ferenka factory in Limerick to make spare parts for *competitors'* products. The judge-made law blocked this, since these competitors would be able to claim infringement of their original drawings for the parts. A rushed amendment to the Copyright Act was introduced to remove this legal obstacle, in total disregard of its negative effect on the capacity of indigenous firms to innovate—a capacity that the state claims stridently is its policy to encourage! The final absurdity was that after Hyster's collapse and departure from the country, the amendment to the law that had been introduced to facilitate them, and for no other purpose, continued onwards through the legislative process![17]

But if intervention cannot enable the country to realise whatever capacity it may have to innovate competitive products, neither can the existing property rights structure. Of the many changes in this that are needed, the one with the most immediately beneficial effect would undoubtedly be to introduce direct protection of innovation along the lines recently studied for the EC by international experts.[18] Its particular implications for Ireland have also been briefly examined.[19]

Ireland became involved in the international patent and trade mark system by subscribing to the Paris Convention in 1925. By doing so it bound itself to treat the nationals of other member-countries in the same way as its own for patent purposes, in exchange, of course, for the same 'national treatment' from them. Although joining the convention resulted in quite new and important property rights of exceptional value, it was never discussed by the Dáil, by the Seanad, *or even by the government.*[20] Its consequences were completely neglected both by politicians and bureaucrats, hell-bent on intervention as they have progressively been since then. But empirical research in TCD has demonstrated what a bad bargain for the country it turned out to be.[21] The international system gives all the advantages to the firms that are at the very cutting edge of all technologies, of which Ireland does not possess a single one. For every £1 of royalty it has brought into the country, at least £100,000 has gone out. Nor has the patent system contributed materially to inward foreign investment, except possibly in the case of pharmaceuticals.[22]

DIRECT PROTECTION OF INNOVATION

Adding arrangements to protect innovation directly to the existing system could do much to redress this imbalance. It would link the grant of protection to local investment. It would ensure that all R&D was done with wholly commercial objectives. It would direct resources towards those who can use them best in innovation, instead of those who have affinities with the bureaucrats who administer any system of public financial aids to industry. Above all, it would stimulate incremental innovation, and innovation of products and components of products that the classical patent system fails to protect.

These are both areas in which Irish industry could hope to be profitably involved. There are countless opportunities in them, in respect of which the first country to introduce direct innovation protection will get a head start. In spite of the Single European Act, such an option is open to individual states of the Community because of article 36 of the Treaty of Rome. Articles 30 to 34 are those that provide for a Community-wide market, unimpeded by national restrictions. However, article 36 derogates from these in respect of industrial and commercial property, provided that this is not used as 'a means of arbitrary discrimination or a disguised restriction on trade between member-states'.

In 1982 the European Court confirmed in respect of designs that, because of article 36, 'in the present state of Community law and in the absence of Community standardisation or of a harmonisation of laws, the determination of the conditions and procedure under which protection . . . is granted is a matter for national rules.'[23] The same ruling was extended to patents by the court in 1988, and amplified in two ways that are important for direct protection of innovation.[24] Firstly, the fact that national and foreign applicants are equal before the patent law was held to dispose of the question whether the discrimination was arbitrary. The same equality is included in the proposals for direct protection of innovation. Secondly, the court held that the objective in legislation 'to foster creative activity on the part of inventors in the interest of industry' saved it from being 'a disguised restriction on trade between member-states'. The whole object of direct protection of innovation, of course, is just such fostering.

These rulings by the European Court confirm that the way is open for the introduction into national laws of direct protection of innovation. If objection were to be raised from any source, the further argument that direct protection of innovation was doing no more than bringing one aspect of intellectual property (the patent system) back to its origins would also have to be considered seriously by the court. Professed readiness to extinguish a national system as soon as direct protection of innovation was introduced on a Community-wide basis would also presumably carry weight with the court, as evidence of restriction of intent to fostering creative activity.

At the Fine Gael 1987 Ard-Fheis the deputy leader and industry spokesman announced his intention of introducing a private member's bill to this effect. If this became law, it could provide an immediate boost to Irish competitiveness.

However, in themselves these new property rights can only ensure that investment and effort are not deprived of rewards by the actions of 'free-riders'. They need to be complemented by arrangements for backing ideas with money. This can never be a rational activity. Uncertainty, not risk, and failure, not success, hold sway here. Nor can these drawbacks be overcome by a portfolio approach, in which a spread of risk results in a few successes paying for many failures. There is persuasive empirical evidence that at the 'ideas' stage, the wider the range of a portfolio the worse the results are likely to be.[25] The rich individuals who so often provided seed capital in the past were able to do so largely because they had no way of knowing how high the odds against them were, but the growth of accountancy and risk analysis techniques has changed all that. Direct public funding of the early stage of innovation has never worked, because what is difficult enough for those who are spending their own money is impossible for an employed investor who is spending someone else's. And, as could be expected, those whose careers are at stake demonstrate remarkable ingenuity in devising means of *avoiding* backing ideas.[26] The situation is not quite hopeless, however, and a radically new approach to this problem that has recently been advanced in an international context has special attractions for countries such as Ireland.[27]

UNITED STATES SBIR PROGRAMME

By far the best source of seed capital in the world at present is the American Small Business Innovation Research Act, 1982. Recognising the wastefulness of public sector R&D, this forces federal agencies that are involved in it to divert part of their budgets (to the extent this year of no less than $400 million) to smaller private firms, in a three-stage competitive award system. In the first instance, awards of $50,000 for six-month feasibility studies go to about one applicant in nine. Second-stage awards, made to about half of the first-stage winners, can be up to $500,000 for two years' work. The third stage is where private venture capital is intended to take over, and in fact prior conditional commitments for such funding are taken into account in the second-stage assessment.

There is an overwhelming case for copying the Small Business Innovation Research (SBIR) scheme in Europe, but it is essential that this be done at the Community, not the national, level, if it is to reach the necessary critical mass.[28] What national governments could do, however, is adapt the SBIR approach to the distribution of funds obtained by increasing the level of fees charged to keep patents and trade marks in force.

In Ireland these are about £1.3 million annually for patents and £0.7 million for trade marks, and at these levels the office covers its costs and passes over about £1.5 million a year to the state.[29] Demand for maintenance of valuable monopolies must be highly inelastic, so that trebling these fees could be expected to produce an additional £3 to 4 million a year to begin with, for a new seed capital fund. More than 99 per cent of this would come from foreign-owned firms, reflecting the extent to which Irish patent and trade mark monopolies benefit them rather than local firms. The financial institutions might be persuaded to match this amount, for two reasons: firstly, much managerial time is spent at present in 'evaluating' proposals that are at far too early a stage to be bankable, and this, together with associated bad debts, could be saved by automatic referral of all such projects to the new fund; and secondly, success of some of the projects will generate demand for conventional finance in the future. A welcome by-product for the banks could be an end to harangues from politicians urging the merit of taking unjustifiable risks with their depositors' money.

A 'SEED CAPITAL FUND'

The Government could also fairly contribute the £1.5 million a year it receives from the Patents Office in return for the vastly greater savings it would make by cutting out public funding of research. Since the 'research' stage of projects is inexpensive compared with what comes later, the resulting total of about £8 million a year, properly used, could hardly fail to lay the foundations for a significant improvement in the competitiveness of Irish products. The fund could pay for the production of prototypes and for subsequent development work on them, on the SBIR model of competitive awards.

Although the money available to the fund would not be raised through taxation (no firm *has* to keep its patents in force, and brands are protected by common law as well as by trade mark registration) it would still be public money, albeit 'diverted'. Consequently, special precautions would have to be taken in the arrangements for its distribution to avoid 'interventionist' values returning by the back door. All decisions about ideas have to be taken on the basis of information that is no better than pre-quantitative, even pre-semantic.

'Meetings of imaginations' are therefore all-important, and the element of peer review, which is standard practice in the natural and social sciences, should dominate the making of awards.

In this context, the 'peers' of applicants would not be bureaucrats or bankers but individuals with actual experience of success (and failure) in innovation. Any committee of such individuals should have a rapidly changing membership, so that ideas can be exposed to the widest possible range of imaginations by repeated applications over a fairly short period. The fund should operate constantly on the basis of objective *and invariably published* research into its own effects (which would be in sharp contrast to the behaviour of the state bodies). And finally, since in an imperfect world any money-distributing agency is in danger from bureaucratic empire-building, its proportion of administrative costs should be pegged to the level of charities that are known to be efficient.

CONCLUSION

Irish enthusiasm for intervention, continued in the face of a record of failure that should have discredited it long ago, is due largely to default. It is not enough to condemn its results without at the same time putting forward practical alternatives in the form of more sophisticated property rights. The two proposals outlined above do this, by offering very much better and virtually costless replacements for some aspects of science and industrial policy. In addition to their specific contribution to improving the productivity of Irish R&D, their successful adoption would show how other aspects of the economy might also be set free.

Notes

1. OECD National Accounts, 1981.
2. L. Franko, *The Threat of Japanese Multinationals,* Chichester: John Wiley 1983, 30.
3. Organisation for Economic Co-operation and Development, *Innovation Policy Ireland,* Paris: OECD 1987.
4. Ibid., 67.
5. See especially Professor David Henderson's outstanding BBC radio talks on 'The Unimportance of Being Right', published in the *Listener,* 27 October–24 November 1977.
6. Richard R. Nelson, *High-Technology Policies: a Five-Nation Study,* Washington: American Enterprise Institute 1984.
7. Stuart Macdonald, 'Theoretically Sound, Practically Useless?: Government Grants for Industrial R&D in Australia' in *Research Policy,* vol. 15 (1986), 269–83.
8. William Kingston, *The Political Economy of Innovation,* the Hague and Boston: Martinus Nijhoff 1984.
9. Douglass North, *Structure and Change in Economic History,* New York: Norton 1981.

10. William Kingston, 'The Lemmings of Democracy' in *Studies,* autumn 1976.
11. William Kingston, 'Ideas, Civil Servants and Keynes' in *Economic Affairs,* January 1983.
12. Advisory Committee on Applied Research and Development, *Exploiting Invention,* London: Cabinet Office 1980, section 25.
13. OECD, *Innovation Policy Ireland,* 58.
14. Finance Act, 1984, S. 16 (2) (*a*) (ii).
15. *British Leyland* v. *Armstrong Patents Ltd.* in the UK; *Alibert* v. *O'Connor* in Ireland.
16. In the Copyright, Patents and Designs Act, 1988.
17. Dáil Debates, 14 October 1987. Mr Desmond O'Malley: '. . . the proposed change in the law to facilitate the proposed Hyster factory in Limerick.'
18. William Kingston (ed.), *Direct Protection of Innovation,* Dordrecht and Boston: Martinus Nijhoff 1987.
19. William Kingston, 'A Patent System to Suit Ireland?' in *Irish Banking Review,* September 1987.
20. All the government minutes for 1925 have been examined, without trace.
21. H. J. P. Murdoch, 'Invention and the Irish Patent System', Trinity College, Dublin, Administrative Research Bureau 1971.
22. Patrick Collins, 'Is the Patent System Relevant to Foreign Investment in Ireland?' (unpublished MBA dissertation, TCD) 1982.
23. *Keurkoop* v. *Nancy Kean Gifts* (case 144/81).
24. *Thetford Corp.* v. *Fiamma SpA* (case 35/87).
25. W. D. Nordhaus, *Invention, Growth and Welfare,* Cambridge (Mass.): MIT Press 1969, 55–6.
26. William Kingston, 'The Financing of New Businesses' in *Industrial Innovation,* London: HMSO for the Cabinet Office 1979.
27. William Kingston, address to the Institute of Patentees and Inventors, in *Future*, April 1988.
28. William Kingston, 'Community R&D Funding: the U.S. shows a Better Way', in *European Affairs*, winter 1988.
29. *Report of the Controller of Patents and Trade Marks for the Year Ending 31 December 1986,* Dublin: Stationery Office (Pl. 4962) 1987.

CORPORATE STRATEGY AND THE COMPETITIVE FACTOR

Leonard Wrigley

University College, Cork

Over the past three decades, Ireland has seen much debate on the uncompetitiveness of its indigenous firms in the traded area, and the consequences overall for economic growth, employment, and the balance of payments. Apart from Ireland's resource deficiency, peripheral location, population growth, and an unhappy history, explanations include excessive wage rates, interest rates, and tax rates; poorly trained managers, technicians, and shop floor workers; crowding out of the traded goods firms by foreign firms, non-traded goods firms, and big government; exclusion from the international market until 1973; entry into the international market in 1973; inadequate investment in technology, marketing, and equipment; and, of course, the class system, with its antagonism between the capitalist class and the working class.

In the face of this baffling array, the temptation presents itself to search for some *deus ex machina* that may be prayed to for a general explanation, such as a conspiracy in 10 Downing Street to keep Irish industry down, the centralisation of economic power in Dublin, or—intellectually more interesting—the inability of the Gael to make common cause against a common enemy: *an dream bocht silte nár chuir le chéile* (the poor ineffective people who did not stand together). While some *deus ex machina* is always attractive, particularly in a land where all adult citizens were reared amidst the established conclusions of a Sinn Féin economic fortress, it seems necessary, before resorting to one or another all-embracing cause, to make an attempt to structure the problem in comparative terms, and to draw at least a rough distinction between, on the one hand, the factors particular to Ireland and, on the other hand, the factors common to all small modern economies.

Apart from Ireland, in the world at large there are ten small modern economies, which we shall call the SMEs. They are small because of a population size (two to eight million) where all citizens can feel part of a family, where all the various social strands can be woven together within a single mind, and where all the important people can know each other, take the measure of each other, and—given shared values and shared information—participate in a consensual decision on matters of state. And they are modern because their people enjoy both a civilised standard of living and a civilised political process, taking 'rule by the wisest and best' (Singapore) as being as civilised as rule by the most.

Broadly, corporate competitiveness is summated by national competitiveness as shown by per capita income, economic growth, and unemployment rates. Many unchangeable things affect competitiveness, for example natural resource endowment, location, population structure, and social history. It is as true as such propositions ever are to say that Ireland is a mid-point amongst SMEs for resources, central/peripheral location, population growth, and happy/unhappy social history, and thus should be a mid-point on changeable things: income, growth, and unemployment. If Ireland is much worse, then the question of competitiveness has to be focused on the strategic variables, such as economic policy, social arrangements, political ideas, and corporate strategies. But where, on the data available, is Ireland actually placed?

TABLE 9.1 **SME Competitiveness in the World at Large**

SME	Pop. (million) 1985	US$ GDP per capita 1985 (at 1985 exchange rate)	GDP growth rate (average 1982–86)	Unemployment (percentage of labour force 1986)	Position on EMF OECD 22-country competitiveness scoreboard
Austria	7.6	8,739	2.1	4.8	12
Denmark	5.1	11,317	3.1	8.5	5
Finland	4.9	11,004	2.5	5.6	10
Hong Kong	5.4*	5,956*	5.6	1.8	—
Ireland	3.5	4,570§	−0.6§	18.8	17
Israel§§	4.3	6,159	1.7	5.4	—
New Zealand	3.3*	7,339*	2.8	5.2	11
Norway	4.2	13,928	3.6	2.5	9
Singapore	2.4*	7,332*	4.5	2.7	—
Sweden	8.4	11,962	2.2	1.7	7
Switzerland	6.5	14,312	1.6	0.9	3

* 1984 (1985 and subsequent data meaningless because of exchange rates)
§ GNP basis (Irish GDP is meaningless because of factor payment)
§§ Israeli data includes 740,000 Arabs (for Jewish people only, population was 3.56 million and GDP per capita was $7,100 in 1985, with a rising trend for each in 1986 and 1987—see EIU, vol. 1, 1988).

Sources: OECD, various dates
Irish data from ESRI, Central Bank, and NESC
Israel, Hong Kong and Singapore data from Economist Intelligence Unit (EIU), various dates
European Management Foundation (EMF) 1986, Competitiveness Report

Facts don't speak for themselves, statistics even less so, particularly financial data across inflation-distorted time or exchange-rate-distorted space. Nevertheless the data in table 9.1 are sufficiently robust to demonstrate that Ireland is the least competitive of all SMEs in per capita income, growth rates, and employment. Why is this so?

A first approximation to an answer may be found in a 1982 report by the Telesis Consulting Group on Irish Industrial Policy. For their study, Telesis subdivided Irish firms according to whether they were in the traded or non-traded area, and whether in natural resources, Irish-owned manufacturing, or foreign-owned manufacturing, as below:

The Telesis Categories

	NATURAL RESOURCES	IRISH MANUFACTURING	FOREIGN MANUFACTURING
TRADED	BUTTER BEEF STOUT	CLOTHING TEXTILES CRYSTAL GLASS	ELECTRONICS CHEMICALS COLA CONCENTRATES
NON-TRADED		CEMENT PACKAGING FURNITURE	

In preparing their report, Telesis made the assumption (which they did not seek to demonstrate) that no country has succeeded in developing a rising standard of living without a host of strong export-oriented, indigenous-owned firms. They dismissed, therefore, the idea—popular in the 1970s—that foreign plants in Ireland could be the pacemakers for Irish industrialisation and export competitiveness. Telesis noted that there were 900 foreign manufacturing plants in Ireland in 1982, which employed 80,000 workers in very well-paid jobs. But Telesis saw these plants as little more than production platforms for tariff-free access from America or elsewhere to the huge EEC market of 320 million population, and for exploiting Irish tax concessions on exports profits. In regard to Irish-owned firms, Telesis observed that food exports 'have resulted chiefly from EEC subsidy'. Correspondingly on manufacturing exports they stated that 'very few indigenous companies . . . had developed an export business which could support an increasing standard of living.' For the non-traded goods firms they took the view that 'the majority of good sized, profitable, successful firms in Ireland are in non-traded business. They have grown rapidly, and they have invested abroad in the same fields as those in which they participated in Ireland.' The Telesis conclusion, simply put, was that Irish firms have not invested to develop new processes or products for the traded area, nor have they made the investment necessary to penetrate new international markets.

The Telesis report constituted a harsh judgement on Irish business enterprise. But the report itself remained largely at the level of description rather than analysis, and the problem of uncompetitiveness of Irish firms is left hanging. The problem has to be confronted analytically. It is not a trivial question why Irish indigenous firms have avoided investment in technology and marketing and, in the first place, have not moved in force towards the international market. Here, for the analysis, we shall use an open systems model of business enterprise. The immediate questions then are, what is the size and structure of the traded area, what are the trends, and what makes for success in the traded area? These questions are answered historically below by looking at the general forces that have shaped and are shaping the flow of international trade.

THE TRADED AREA

In the world at large, the traded area consists of the totality of the markets in each country open to competition from imports. It is not a fixed area.

The pattern of world trade has been changing over time. In 1913 only 50 per cent of the exports of industrial countries went to other industrial countries; by 1955 the proportion was 63 per cent, and by 1973 it was 75 per cent. The implications are quite clear: increasingly the main customers of one industrial country are the other industrial countries.

What is enormously important is that since the Second World War, under the financial umbrella of the Bretton Woods Agreement, the world traded area increased relative to the world non-traded area as well as grew vastly in size. From 1948 to 1973 world trade grew at 10 per cent per year, while world output grew at 5 per cent. There was then a slow-down, which was connected immediately with the oil shock of 1973 but ultimately with the limitations of the Bretton Woods umbrella for a more complex world. Since 1973 trade and output have grown in parallel, about 2 per cent per year, though for manufacturing only world trade has expanded annually at 5 per cent, world manufacturing output at half that rate. Because of this expansion in the traded area, particularly for manufacturing, firms in small economies that were open were able to surmount the limitations of a small domestic market. This was a development of the first importance. Small economies could specialise in what they are good at, by exporting the products for which they had a comparative advantage to the world at large.

The opportunity for increased specialisation, and the associated economies of scale, was of course the great advantage offered by an expanding traded area. Adam Smith, in his famous dictum 'The division of labour is limited by the extent of the market', was quite simply expressing the most important proposition in all economies. The greater specialisation of firms in the 1950s and 1960s, within a stable financial framework, was the economic basis for the golden years of the world in general, small economies in particular.

It has been argued that a large domestic market gives firms a competitive advantage: the larger the home market the greater the advantage. The assumption is that firms best learn the economies of scale at home. The European Management Forum, for example, in its 1986 *World Competitiveness Report*, stated: 'In the industrialised countries, a large population is clearly a competitive advantage. It provides a large domestic market, offering economies of scale in production . . .'[1]

TABLE 9.2 **Share in Value of 'World' Exports in Manufacturing, 1950–80 (per cent)**

	1950	1960	1970	1980*
United States	27.3	21.6	18.5	16.0
Japan	3.4	6.9	11.7	13.6
UK	25.5	16.5	10.8	9.7
France	9.9	9.6	8.7	10.5
Germany	7.3	19.3	19.8	20.8
Italy	4.0	5.1	7.2	8.3
Smaller countries	22.6	21.0	23.3	21.3

* Same data for 1979. Sources: as table 9.1.

Much the same argument was put forward in Ireland during the debate on the Single European Act. Historical data on market share of world exports in manufacturing does not support this argument. Table 9.2 shows no particular relationship between population size and the trend in market share. The real factors surely are the liberalisation of trade, and the supply-side capability of economies, big, small, and in-between.

It can indeed be argued that firms in small economies do have a comparative advantage if their economy is truly open. If a firm, when young, acquires the habit of exporting, it will export naturally in mature years. It is necessary to see that the most important assets of a firm are informational, the essence of which are the 'core skills', namely *the collective information acquired through collective activity in a competitive market, not just of a market and a technology but of the potential in one in relation to the potential in the other*, as is portrayed in fig. 9.1. In the large, the core skill reflects the habits, traditions and culture that were developed when the firm was young, in its most formative years.

In that light, people coming together to start a firm (or a new product division in an existing firm) in a small modern economy will, if they are ambitious for long-term growth, naturally, from the beginning, search throughout the world for marketing information,

FIG. 9.1

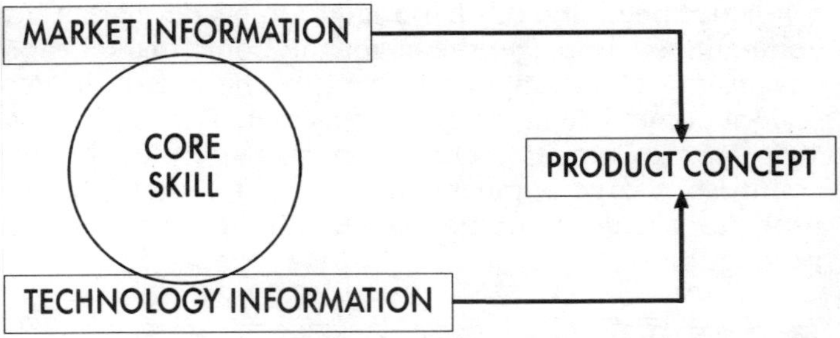

as well as for technology information. The result will be the development of core skills in designing and producing a world-wide product acceptable immediately to world-wide customers. There is good statistical evidence for this argument, including research by Killing, Murphy, Hennessy, and Levie.[2] And a recent article by Porter in the *Harvard Business Review* is completely in accord with this line of reasoning.

We now return to table 9.2. The data show that the United States lost market share. The reason is germane. The United States emerged from the Second World War as the undisputed world leader in technology and marketing skills. In effect, American firms became the brand leaders in one market after another. Accordingly, the dollar became highly valued. Many American firms then found it more profitable to transfer capital assets abroad, in order to serve export markets through local production, than to export to these markets from plants in the United States.

At the same time, the American firms became vulnerable in their domestic market. With rising affluence and expectations, the world market, including the traded area in the United States, was segmenting. The professional class as well as the poor were emerging as distinct market segments. American firms became vulnerable in the new segments.

They were vulnerable because of the standardisation and mass production of their product lines as required for world-wide products on the central market position. They were vulnerable to an assault by firms in developed small countries that differentiated their product by superior design and quality control, and who targeted the professional-class customers for consumer or producer goods, with a carefully focused strategy. They were also vulnerable to firms in developing small countries that targeted below the line with a strategy of the lowest price at the point of sale. All these firms were targeting the vulnerable gaps that were opening off-centre, as portrayed in fig. 9.2, which positions products by price and service.

Another phenomenon was also occurring that helped these firms, apart from market segmentation. Because American firms were the brand leaders they were vulnerable to the 'catch up' strategy of those firms that could challenge them in speed of development of the

FIG. 9.2

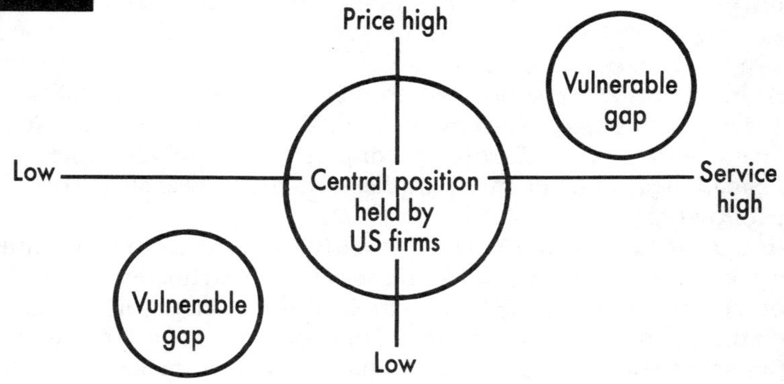

relevant technology. Indeed the very distance to the technological frontier, as set by American firms, created an opportunity for unusually fast growth by firms in the small modern economies as these firms speeded to catch up in technology. In the very process of closing the distance between themselves and the American firms, they were stretching themselves and therefore strengthening their informational assets for increasing the pace. They were, indeed, in a virtuous circle.

The critical factor in filling the vulnerable gaps was the speed with which the firms could both design a superior product and improve production technology, especially direct labour productivity. Speed was also important in developing an expertise in marketing precisely and effectively to that position where the vulnerable gap existed. The challenge was to get a whole set of economically useful things moving quickly and in harmonious relationship. If we take product quality to mean value in use to the consumers and value added by the producer, then the critical success factor in securing market share for a newly emerged off-centre segment in the traded area was speed in developing product quality, marketing effectiveness, and direct labour productivity. Obviously, speed called for a large investment in informational assets, hence success in the traded area was limited to those firms that had access to risk finance—and were prepared to risk it.

COMPETITIVE FACTORS: (1) PRODUCT QUALITY AND MARKETING

A flea is not a scaled-down elephant: it is another species of animal. Difference in scale means difference in kind. The logic of an elephant is power; of a flea it is hustle.

Hustle characterises the economic strategy of all the prosperous small modern economies. Their economic and social system has so developed that each can reallocate resources across markets and institutions at great speed (and with near-'Arrow-Debreu' efficiency) to respond quickly to an external shock so as to maintain competitiveness, financial stability, economic growth, and full employment. These economies are most themselves, they are most in accord with their inner springs of action, when they hustle in consensual union to ward off a threat from an environmental discontinuity or to exploit a great opportunity suddenly opening up in the world market.

Small means hustle, but it implies something else also. Consider the following:

—In 1820, when cheap English textiles threatened age-old community skills and craftsmanship, Zürich businessmen hustled to develop precision textile machinery, which they targeted for up-market textile producers. Over time, Zürich became synonymous with precision engineering, and remains so—with associated institutes and skills—to the present time.

—In 1946, with the advent of Soviet war repatriation claims, Finland's up-country businessmen, to avert the catastrophe of foreign occupation, hustled to develop heavy-duty transport equipment, such as dockside container cranes, off-the-road high-mobility grader trucks, nuclear-powered ice-breaker tugs, and mobile telephones for difficult terrain, all of which were efficient down to 60 below zero and with unskilled labour. In the result, Finland became the world centre for Arctic-type transport and communications equipment, and remains so.

—In 1974, when the oil price shock threatened Denmark's energy-hungry economy, Jutland's businessmen hustled to develop a new cheese, Feta—like that from goat's milk—for oil-rich Arabia. At near-lightning speed, 5,000 specially designed refrigerated trucks were constructed to move the newly developed Feta cheese from Jutland's dairy enterprises to Tehran and all points south. Denmark is now world leader for speciality cheese exports to the Middle East.

These examples show how small economies can hustle to match the potential in their existing stock of technology to the potential in the market. What is important is that these countries focused on familiar areas: they did not start from a blank sheet of paper. The central economic characteristic of prosperous small modern economies is, in short: focused hustle.

We are concerned to identify the competitive factors critical for success in small modern economies. It is necessary that the factors identified be inescapably linked to product quality, marketing effectiveness and labour productivity for products targeted with focused hustle to an off-centre market position. What are these factors?

The most obvious competitive factor that presented itself in field studies to Irish researchers (UCC MBA and MBS candidates, whose practical experience included senior management positions in Irish business enterprises) was a mass of export-experienced business firms.

Compared with Ireland, other small modern economies are richly endowed with business firms of all sizes, many of them established a hundred years ago and more. These business firms were export-oriented. Even small firms in low-technology industry, for example Denmark's furniture firms, can and do export. All the firms are well endowed with professional people who work together and who have got to know each other well and have evolved a 'core skill' to compete in the market.

Connected with the firms is a self-conscious business class in which export orientation, commercial creativity and a spirit of entrepreneurship are strongly embedded. According to the researchers' field reports, in certain respects—for example in getting things done through people—this business class is more self-assured than its Irish counterpart. This self-assurance, arguably, can be traced historically to the fact that in these other countries, landlords and peasants were of the same race. Be that as it may, there is an immediately striking difference between the business leaders in the other small economies and those in Ireland. The business leaders in the other economies were from the traded area, in Ireland the business leaders are from the non-traded area. Those who organise production and shape public opinion are export-oriented (and multilingual) in other small modern economies. In Ireland, the business leaders have tended, at least until recently, to be inward-looking. The difference translates into business stance in regard to product quality, marketing effectiveness and direct labour production for an off-centre market position and to financial interest in a high or a low valuation of the national currency on the exchange.

Also associated with the business firms are business schools, universities and other institutes for transferring and assimilating economically useful information. These schools and colleges developed and acquired their identity from the industry or specific range of industries in which the economy specialised. Indeed, the largest corporations, such as Nestlé's of Switzerland, serve as a major finance source for a particular business school or technical institute.

Export-oriented business firms, an export-oriented business class and business-oriented universities and schools constitute, as it were, the framework conditions for the recruitment of highly talented youth into export industry, and the formation of their intellectual capital. Supporting this framework condition is a social ethos in which this kind of work and focus makes a good career. In the prosperous small modern economies, a lifetime of work involving main life energies in product design, production technology and marketing is seen as a good thing. The educational system is set up that way, so are the firms, and so are the various performance and reward systems.

As an illustration, the Danish equivalent of an Irish 26-pointer (NUI scoring system) interested in dairy foods marketing will go to Århus School of Business for his undergraduate education; upon completion he is likely to work for four or five years in the dairy industry of New Zealand, then undertake an MBA programme at a major American business school before returning to Århus for a marketing position, perhaps in Dairy Denmark, which is structured to place him where his interests and talents can be usefully employed. Part of his career will include experience in an R&D unit and a production unit, so he gets to know well the colleagues upon whose success his success depends. In all this, it is the structured nature of high-talented careers in business that is noteworthy.

The contrast with Ireland is quite glaring. The Irish 26-pointer will go for medicine or law, where, indeed, he will have a structured career and good pay. People will respond to economic incentives for the improvement of themselves. In Ireland, medicine and law take the cream.

We can see that, from the eyes of competent Irish researchers, the factors making for corporate competitiveness in the traded area are export-experienced business firms, an export-oriented business class, business-oriented schools and universities, and a performance and reward system that attracts highly talented youth towards a career in export business.

In the prosperous small economies the business firms, business class and associated universities reflect—and embellish—a comparative advantage that has been developed in the economy over time, which takes the shape of a set of related industries. This comparative advantage may originally have been based on raw materials, climate, or location, but has evolved over the years into a massive stock of intellectual capital, of shared, economically useful information about the set of related industries and associated technologies and markets. Each country is of course unique in its stock of intellectual capital. At the same time there are similarities in intellectual capital between all those economies originally strongly endowed with natural resources, and between all those that always were resource-deficient and therefore forced to rely upon human skills for their economic development, as well as between all those that are making economic progress centrally as the gateway between major economic systems.

Accordingly, each of the eleven small modern economies may be classified as follows:

(1) *Resource-led:* Austria, New Zealand, Norway, Sweden.
(2) *Skill-led:* Denmark, Finland, Israel, Switzerland.
(3) *Gateway:* Hong Kong, Singapore, Ireland.

Of course this classification if pressed becomes simplistic, and ultimately absurd. But if not an aid to minute analysis, neither can it be ignored entirely. It does represent a point of view from which economic behaviour can be seen and compared, and the overall effect noted in the ratio of total trade (imports plus exports) to GDP, and relative competence in product quality and marketing effectiveness, as in table 9.5.

TABLE 9.3

Product Quality: Ranking of the eleven SMEs (amongst 22 OECD countries)

	Product design, styling, & packaging*	Ranking	Product safety*	Ranking	On-time delivery of products*	Ranking	Search for technology§	Ranking
Resource-led								
Austria	62.73	11	80.91	6	74.09	7	55.81	18
New Zealand	63.75	10	78.75	8	57.50	13	68.75	3
Norway	57.78	16	78.67	9	66.67	10	60.89	14
Sweden	75.64	6	88.73	1	76.73	5	68.00	4
Skill-led								
Denmark	91.50	1	82.00	5	79.50	4	68.00	4
Finland	76.67	5	70.95	11	65.71	11	63.33	10
Israel								
Switzerland	72.29	8	85.06	3	82.65	3	65.54	9
Gateway								
Hong Kong	65.00		53.50		81.50		70.50	
Singapore	61.38		67.59		77.24		64.83	
Ireland	46.22	21	48.00	18	40.00	20	53.64	19

*Ranking: 0 (very bad) to 100 (very good).
§Ranking: 0 (inefficient) to 100 (efficient).
Source: as table 9.1

Clearly, from table 9.3, Ireland is last on the list, that is, is assessed on the data to be the least competitive in product quality. Why is Ireland in this condition for crucial variables? The reason is that Ireland kept itself cut off from the expanding traded area for two decades after the end of the Second World War by tariff walls and then, from 1973, by an overvalued currency. It has not been moved to specialise, focus and hustle to develop a related set of world-wide products targeted at off-centre positions in the traded area.[3]

The human mind is so constructed that only through extraordinary effort—and, perhaps, the stimulus of a catastrophe—can it surmount the established conclusions amidst which it has been reared. All adult Irishmen in Ireland, and their parents, have been reared on the established conclusions of an economic fortress, namely self-sufficiency, centralised government, and general handymanship. These were the governing ideas from the moment of the foundations of the state in 1922.

Fundamentally, Ireland in its most formative years accepted uncritically the infant industry theory of Hamilton (and List). This is where the intellectual roots of Ireland's competitiveness problem lies. Implicit in that theory is the logic of a young, resource-rich country like the United States in Hamilton's day: 1776. What America needed when young was a host of import-substitution firms. But Ireland is a small resource-deficient country. What Ireland needed in this century was not import-substitution firms; Ireland needed export-oriented firms, which may be infants at the start and, like all infants, needing help—such as, for example, an undervalued currency (allied to restrictions on foreigners acquiring Irish assets). That was not what Ireland got. It got, under the banner of Sinn Féin, an Arthur Griffith version of Frederick List. Sinn Féin did great harm to the development of export firms sharply focused on particular segments of the world market.

COMPETITIVE FACTORS: (2) LABOUR PRODUCTIVITY

Within favourable industrial framework conditions, the factors making for labour productivity in the prosperous small modern economies are apprenticeship training, investment in equipment, and management quality. But the methodology of determining labour wages is very much a background factor in labour productivity, and also merits attention here.

Generally speaking, apprenticeship training for labour skills follows completion of secondary school. Apprentices are taken on as such by business firms, and trained by craftsmen on the shop floor; that is, apprenticeship is learning by example and by doing. The period varies according to trade: four years is typical for important crafts. While under training, the apprentice attends, part-time, the relevant vocational school. In all this, trade unions may be directly involved. The apprenticeship period is rigorous: very much so in Switzerland, but community-supported.

In all small modern economies there is a strong tendency towards improving labour productivity by improved capital equipment. The reason for this is to offset a shortage of skilled labour. But with modern equipment, including robots, the machine has proved more reliable, more consistent, than human nature. Thus the use of equipment is part of a movement to improve product quality.

TABLE 9.4 **SME Relative Wages, Productivity and Gross Investment, 1984**

	Comparative take-home pay, metal-worker, 1984, PPP*	Actual hourly pay level for production worker in US$, 1984	Real GDP per employee in US$, 1984	Gross domestic investment as percentage, GDP/GNP, 1984
Resource-led				
Austria	10.07	6.47	15,573	22.4
New Zealand	10.41	4.65	15,968	22.8
Norway	14.03	10.35	20,065	25.1
Sweden	11.85	9.15	16,045	18.6
Skill-led				
Denmark	17.62	8.09	15,733	16.9
Finland	12.41	7.65	14.809	24.3
Israel	–	–	–	–
Switzerland	13.41	9.56	27,393	23.3
Gateway				
Hong Kong	3.05	1.60	9,194	26.6
Singapore	3.25	2.43	12,397	46.8§
Ireland	11.82	5.46	9,720§§	24.3

* Hourly pay in German marks, adjusted for purchasing power parity.
§ Including the Central Provident Fund (CPF) state pension investments.
§§ GNP: see footnote, table 9.1
Source: see table 9.1.

What is important is not just capital formation but also its direction. Here there is evidence of real differences between the other small economies and Ireland. Much of the capital investment in Ireland during the past few decades seems not to have been productive, in the sense of leading to new products or to market creation. Irish investment money seems to have been wasted on attempts to keep marginal businesses alive. In the result, Irish labour productivity does not reflect Irish capital investment. By contrast, labour productivity in the other small economies does relate to the level of capital.

But there is more than that. SMEs, such as Sweden, spend huge money on R&D to stabilise the design of a new product before the product is launched. They then spend huge money on process technology to stabilise the production method and equipment. In this way labour becomes experienced from the moment of product launch: the learning curve is steepened, and direct labour productivity rises fast as experience accumulates. This investment strategy requires excellence in management skills.

Management quality is indeed a factor in labour productivity, both directly, in the capability of getting things done through people, and indirectly, in shaping the direction of capital formation. In UCC Management Department research on labour productivity and on change-over in technology, the Irish managers in the foreign branch plants came out ahead—just ahead—of their counterparts in two other small European economies, Denmark and Switzerland. The quality of Irish managers in foreign branch plants, particularly in chemicals, drugs, and electronics was quite remarkable (as indeed was labour productivity). The management of the parent companies in the United States were contacted: they were not surprised by the result. They had already seen the Irish plants as the most efficient in their world-wide activities.

By contrast, the management quality in traditional Irish manufacturing firms was, characteristically, far below their counterparts abroad. There were exceptions, and important exceptions, but the generality remains valid. Clearly, the average Irish managers could learn from the best of Irish managers. So far they seem not to have done this. The problem of Irish labour productivity may be the difficulty of the average Irish manager in assimilating information from a person who is of the same race as himself.

COMPETITIVE FACTORS: (3) WAGES

Wages are the crucial factor in cost competitiveness. In commodity production, indeed, labour is the key cost factor. However, while the price of production materials and investment money do not differ greatly from one country to another, labour wages do vary enormously.

In the prosperous small modern economies, because of the huge size of the traded sector, labour wages are treated as a residue. Given a fixed exchange rate, the price of manufacturing goods in the traded area will be constant. Wage increases within a firm that are not offset by production or import prices will cut profit margins, and eventually eliminate the firm. This may not be in anyone's interest; yet labour wages have to be set from time to time. The negotiators use a model to help the negotiations to be fruitful.

The Swedish model, which is followed by many, has wage increases determined by average productivity growth across all industry sectors. This system (idealised here) compels attention to changes in productivity and in export prices. Firms—and sectors—that lose competitiveness are eliminated, compelling labour to move to where productivity and/or traded goods prices have increased. In practice, exchange rates are adjusted from time to time to maintain balance, including full employment. There are variations of this model to account for variations in willingness of labour to move from a locality; but the general principle is the same: labour wages are treated as the residue.

Ireland is different. Ireland and the UK constitute one labour market. English and Irish wage rates correspond closely. Because England is larger, it sets the wage rate for the market as a whole. In Ireland the results seem quite remarkable when placed against Irish labour output. It seems even more remarkable on a comparative 'take-home pay' basis when adjustments are made for purchasing power parity. On that basis an Irish metal-worker gets more than his counterparts in Austria, and about the same as his counterparts in Sweden. This is despite differences in real output, as can be seen in table 9.4. Ireland has a competitive problem in regard to the relationship between wage rates and output.

The problem is greater when labour relations are taken into account. In a study for the present paper by Tony Barlow, the strike record, year by year, of Irish workers was worse than for four other small modern economies for which reliable data were available.

In other small modern economies, labour wage is a variable. Wages are not a factor, at least not a long-run factor, in competitiveness. By contrast, in Ireland labour wages are a long-run factor. Product prices are determined in Ireland not by world competition but by Irish wage costs. But these wage costs are set in England.

CORPORATE STRATEGY

For present purposes, corporate strategy is the pattern of executive decisions that determines how the firm is to compete in its environment, and what it is and is to be in product-market relationships, capital assets, and informational assets. Corporate strategy is importantly influenced by three things: first, the size and structure of the market outside the firm; second, the stock and flow of informational assets within the firm; and third, the cost structure of inputs to the firm. These are portrayed in fig. 9.3, with the essence of corporate strategy spelt out.

FIG. 9.3

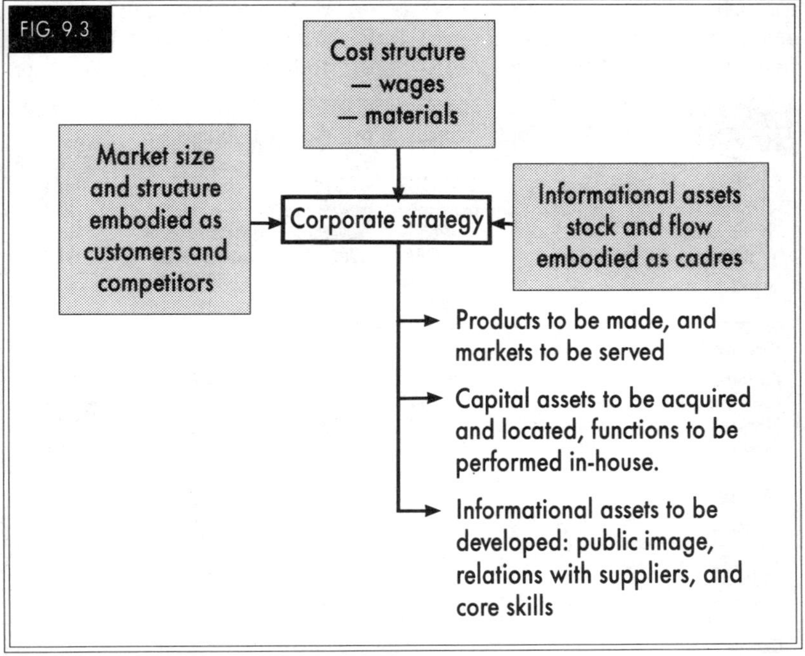

The generic strategies open to the firm can be seen along two dimensions: first, whether to compete on lowest cost or on differentiated products; second, whether to focus on a single product or, alternatively, to diversify into related products or unrelated products, as below, with examples from Ireland:

	Single product	**Related product**	**Unrelated product**
Lowest-cost product	CRH Irish Esso	Goodman Kerry	FMC Jones
Differentiated product	Barry's Tea GPA	Smurfit Glen Dimplex	Glanmire Industries Fitzwilton

Broadly, the more capital-intensive (and also the smaller) the firm, the greater the tendency to be single-product; correspondingly, the larger the firm, and the more the firm is science-based, the greater the tendency towards a related-product strategy. Also, broadly, the higher the wages, the greater the tendency to compete on differentiated products.

The unrelated (or conglomerate) strategy is, essentially, a hangover from the 'golden years', when competition was low, financial markets were inefficient and many firms in small modern economies, including Ireland, acquired whatever business was going, for an attractive price. Waterford and Guinness are examples in Ireland of firms that used that strategy in some of their acquisitions in the past.

TABLE 9.5 **SME Competitiveness in the World at Large**

SME countries by economic strategy	Pop. (million) 1985	UD$ GDP per capita 1985 (at 1985 exchange rate)	GDP growth rate (average 1982–86)	Unemployment (percentage of labour force, 1986)	Trade/ GDP ratio, 1987
Resource-led					
Austria	7.6	8,739	2.1	4.8	0.56
New Zealand	3.3*	7,339*	2.8	5.2	0.50
Norway	4.2	13,928	3.6	2.5	0.54
Sweden	8.4	11,962	2.2	1.7	0.53
Skill-led					
Denmark	5.1	11,317	3.1	8.5	0.44
Finland	4.9	11,004	2.5	5.6	0.47
Israel §§	4.3	6,159	1.7	5.4	0.59
Switzerland	6.5	14,312	1.6	0.9	0.59
Gateway					
Hong Kong	5.4*	5,956*	5.6	1.8	1.4
Singapore	2.4*	7,332*	4.5	2.7	2.6
Ireland	3.5	4,570§	−0.6§	18.8	1.2§

* 1984 (1985 and subsequent data meaningless because of exchange rate)
§ GNP basis (Irish GDP is meaningless because of factor payment)
§§ Israeli data includes 740,000 Arabs (for Jewish people only, population was 3.56 million and GDP per capita was $7,100 in 1985, with a rising trend for each in 1986 and 1987 – see EIU, vol. 1, 1988).

SOURCES: OECD, various dates.
Irish data from ESRI, Central Bank, and NESC.
Israel, Hong Kong and Singapore data from Economist Intelligence Unit (EIU), various dates.
European Management Foundation (EMF) 1986, Competitiveness Report.

That was some years ago. There are still conglomerate firms around, but they are a dying breed, unable to survive under severe competition. We can confine our attention, therefore, to single-product and related-product strategies. Unless otherwise mentioned, all firms in small economies can be seen to use a differentiated-product strategy. We follow the order in table 9.5.

In producer-led countries, the characteristic firm is large and tends, since the 1960s, towards the related-product strategy. The reason for this strategy is the enormous increase in the cost of research for product improvement. 'Relatedness' in product line essentially means that the core skills appertaining to one product can be transferred to another product to give that other product a competitive advantage. Relatedness therefore implies that the activities involved in the various products of the firms are sufficiently similar to enable the sharing of core skills to be meaningful. With a related-product strategy, the cost of a huge investment to improve the design of one product can be spread over all the other products. Firms such as Volvo, which needs to spend huge sums to keep car design up to competitive standards, have a strong incentive to adopt a corporate strategy of related products: for example, to include trucks and engines in its product line.

In skill-led countries the characteristic firm is small to medium-sized and tends to be single-product or closely related product. Many of the firms in Denmark, Israel and Switzerland are essentially 'job shops', where the shop floor workers are skilled craftsmen, and such firms tend to be labour-intensive and skill-intensive. When, for example, in Switzerland, a firm is custom-making a 64,000-horse-power diesel engine, fuel-efficient for a torrid region in Brazil, the skill requirements are quite enormous. These 'job shop' firms also are extraordinarily responsive to market conditions. This is particularly true for Israeli high-technology firms such as Tadiron Electronics and Iscar Tools, where the various markets swing wildly. Finland is something of an exception: the characteristic firm there is large, presumably because it is likely to have its roots in war repatriation work for the Soviet Union from 1946 to 1960.

With the European small economies the projected single European market naturally has impacted greatly on corporate strategy. The response of firms has been to acquire other closely related product firms within the EEC. For example Kalmer, the Swedish fork-lift truck manufacturer, acquired the UK fork-lift truck firm Coventry Climax and installed its own engineering staff to transfer Kalmer's core skills to bring Coventry Climax up to Swedish standards. The corporate goal of such firms is to dominate the EEC market segment in which they are becoming established, and to do this by enhancing research capabilities in their homeland, and to buy up competitors within the EEC. Essentially their strategy has changed from exporting the actual product to exploiting the rents from their informational assets.

The corporate strategy of firms in the Pacific Rim gateway countries tends to be single-product, low-cost. For example the textile firms in Hong Kong confine themselves to a limited product range, and rely upon labour wages of about $1.80 per hour to compete in the low end of the US multiple store business. However, these Hong Kong firms can be capital-intensive, using electronic V-belt knitters to ensure flexibility. Naturally the corporate strategy of firms in Hong Kong is designed to exploit Hong Kong's status of duty-free access to US markets. Much the same applies to firms in Singapore.

This account of corporate strategy in the prosperous small modern economy would be incomplete without reference to three other aspects. Firstly, the government makes no direct effort to influence corporate strategy. For illustration, these other economies do not have the array of detailed industrial programmes that have been so common in Ireland since 1964. Secondly, businessmen in these countries will foray into a highly competitive arena, both as a reconnaissance in force and to develop the informational assets of the firm. And thirdly, physical assets *per se* seem not to be greatly valued. What are highly valued are informational assets. A successful firm like Dairy Denmark in Århus would see its informational assets as constituting perhaps 70 per cent of its wealth.

IRELAND

In looking at corporate strategy in Ireland, we concentrate on the Irish dairy co-operatives and on Irish firms in traded manufacturing products. We will, however, take occasion to glance at Irish firms in the non-traded area. We see no point in considering the foreign-owned branch plants, since most remain as production platforms, and the exceptions exhibit no clear pattern.

With six exceptions, the fifty dairy co-operatives in Ireland are truncated businesses, lacking any semblance to a core skill, and generally incapable of developing new products for export. There are three reasons for this truncation: firstly, CAP intervention price support kept butter-making profitable; secondly, marketing is organisationally separated from technology; and thirdly, dairy management is dominated by farmer representations. Most dairy co-operatives have no marketing departments at all. They just make butter and then transfer it to Bord Bainne, the central marketing board. Moreover, the organisational structure of the Irish dairy co-operatives is mechanical: any attempt towards new product development would be difficult, and meet with hostility. The corporate strategy of dairy co-operatives, therefore, is oriented to producing butter, and associated skim-milk powder, and this at lowest cost.

The six dairy co-operatives that are the exceptions are quite large (sales around £200 million a year), with good technology and fair market skills. All six have a corporate strategy of related differentiated products; two of them in fact have organised new product development units, and already produced important new export products that are competing effectively in the UK.

The Irish manufacturers in the traded area have been harshly assessed by Telesis. The strategy of these Irish firms is low-cost; most of them were rooted in protectionism, and have only just survived under the very different conditions of the traded area of an open economy. The Telesis Report characterised Ireland as a country with few high-skilled, high-technology enterprises; where industry's exports were small and confined to a limited range of markets; where Irish firms were not able to meet the sub-supply needs of foreign firms; where small firms existed chiefly in low-skilled activities in which competition from abroad was absent. But Telesis noted that there were important exceptions.

The corporate strategy of Irish firms in the non-traded area has been—apart from the cement producer—related, differentiated products. Including the cement producer, all these firms tend to be quite large and profitable. They are so in Ireland. Moreover, as their scale of operations reached the limit of the economy, many of these firms transferred assets abroad, and competed in other countries, such as the United States and UK. The question must be faced: why is there this difference between Irish firms in the traded and the non-traded area? The obvious explanation is the high real cost exchange rate regime in Ireland, which works in favour of firms in the non-traded area.

In fact, with Irish manufacturing firms in the traded area whose corporate strategy was differentiated products, for example McGee with quality suits, Glen Dimplex with quality heaters, and Biocon with special enzymes, the firms have done well. Moreover, they have done well against fierce competition from other countries. Here it is important to note that these firms are not rooted in protectionism. They were created with an export orientation. Moreover, they use the best equipment. Their labour productivity is high. In this way, they have surmounted the obstacles of an overvalued exchange rate. But the number of such firms remains very few relative, say, to Denmark, though the number is growing year by year.

It seems necessary to emphasise again that there was a limitation in the infant industry argument of Hamilton. The argument was limited to young, resource-rich, potentially large economies. In such economies, infant firms can emerge, develop, and mature, and increasingly enjoy the economies of scale and of experience. As they mature they compete with each other in the domestic market. On moving towards the export market, they do so with strength, experience, and skill, and also with plenty of money. The firms in Ireland that emerged in the 1930s, during the early days of protectionism, developed and matured without getting to that size where economies of scale were practical. It was unreasonable to expect in 1973 that such 40-year-old firms could respond effectively to a hundredfold increase in market size. They simply didn't have the crucial informational assets.

IMPLICATIONS FOR GOVERNMENT

Competitiveness means the ability of a country to earn its standard of living in competition with other countries. The emphasis is on 'earn'. In the language of Bruce Scott, 'a rising standard of living from foreign borrowings does not imply increased competitiveness.'

Ireland has not earned its standard of living since 1973. It has acquired bad habits, amongst the worst of which is an unwillingness to confront uncomfortable truths. But one truth must be confronted now: Irish indigenous industry is in no shape to be ready for the single European market projected for 1992.

It might be ready by 1998, if major changes are effected in the meantime. These changes relate to the role of the Government, the exchange rate, export business amalgamation, and reorientation of higher education to embrace catch-up technology and professional-level adult education. These are considered in turn below.

There is no evidence from the success of small modern countries that, within the framework of a mixed economy, the government has any particular capacity to determine competitiveness, rates of economic growth, or employment. There is no evidence that state control over industrial investment produced a more efficient allocation of resources. On the contrary, the very success of countries like Switzerland, where central government is small, implies a limited role for government in relation to business.

Within that limited role, however, the government can be important. Here we come to the price system. In a small economy, good information about the economic world is critical for competitiveness. The essential role of the price system is to convey economically useful information from the environment to the firm. If that system is distorted, then the information is distorted. The central role of the exchange rate is to guide the allocation of resources. If the exchange is overvalued, resources—including entrepreneurs—are moved towards the non-traded area. The prosperity of the non-traded area relative to the traded area in Ireland strongly implies an overvalued exchange rate.

There is another aspect. Given that nominal wages are sticky, any downturn in market conditions means either that the exchange rate falls or that unemployment increases. Of course, a devaluation may lead to inflation. The experience of the Nordic countries is that the inflation is slight.

Ireland should devalue the pound. There is nothing else of comparable importance it can do to move resources towards exports. In the end, we are talking about our best people becoming rich by exporting.

Over a period, the above moves will lead to a more competitive economy. New business firms will then have had time to grow. Ireland has not got this time. Hence, the amalgamation route to growth must be encouraged by enabling legislation. The key concept is relatedness: the capacity of one firm to transfer its competitive skills to another firm in a meaningful way.

Three rules for determining the usefulness of acquisition for the purpose of transferring skills are:

(1) The activities involved in the business are similar enough for the sharing of expertise;

(2) The transfer of skills involves activities important to competitive advantage;
(3) The skills transferred represent a significant source of competitive advantage.

These should assist successful firms in the non-traded area to move towards the traded area by the methods of amalgamation. That is the route to follow.

In all this, the universities and technology institutes have an important role. There is no reason to continue educating highly talented youth for careers that are not there. There is need to help Ireland catch up with best practices elsewhere. This implies a role of bringing useful knowledge across the frontier. There is also need for more high-class adult education, such as one-year executive diplomas in management, for those managers with no formal education now.

An overall improvement in corporate competitiveness, like an improvement in the rate of economic development, means doing things differently. It means learning new ways of doing eonomically useful things. This takes time, for it involves the accumulation of informational assets. People, of course, can be told what should be done. But that does not mean they will learn, if only because they do not know what the words mean for them in a collective context. But Ireland can speed up the process of accumulating informational assets by good government policies, as have been put in place since 1987.

Notes

1. European Management Reports, OECD Reports, EIU Reports, various dates, 1980–8.
2. UCC Management Department MBA and MBS theses, 1980–8.
3. Leonard Wrigley, 'Ireland in Economic Space', in Joseph Lee (ed.) *Ireland: a Sense of Place*, Cork: Cork University Press 1985.

10

TOWARDS A STRATEGY FOR COMPETITIVENESS

Dermot McAleese

'It is vital, if the economy is to realise its full potential, especially on the employment front, that the progress made to date in resolving the basic imbalances in the economy and strengthening its overall competitiveness should be sustained.'[1]

Significant improvements in competitiveness have occurred during the years 1987 and 1988. The progress referred to in the above quotation from the White Paper really has happened:

— inflation has fallen to 2 per cent in 1988, the lowest rate in thirty years;

— the current balance of payments has improved from a deficit of 15 per cent of GNP in 1981 to a surplus of 4 per cent in 1988, a turn-around of historic proportions;

— Government borrowing, which a short time ago seemed to be locked in to a frightening 13 per cent of GNP, looks set to fall to about 6 per cent in 1988;

— hourly earnings in manufacturing in 1988 are expected to increase by 4 per cent, a significantly lower rate than in the UK and broadly in line with the EMS average;

— interest rates have fallen to a level close to the ECU rate and, in mid-1988, were three percentage points below the comparable UK rates.

These broad advances in the macroeconomic position have been reinforced by policy measures at a micro level. There have been structural reforms in the telecommunications industry that have led to greater efficiency and lower (relative) prices. Public-sector transport companies are operating in a less regulated, more competitive environment, and the consumer has benefited through steep price reductions. Dublin-to-London air fares have fallen by between 48 and 66 per cent for peak and off-peak travel, respectively, between pre-May 1986 and summer 1988.[2] Electricity prices to industry are now regarded as generally competitive, a remarkable change in the position of a few years ago. Marginal income tax rates have been cut—the highest rate from 65 per cent to 58 per cent—and artificial cross-border activities induced by tax differentials have been curbed by tax and administrative changes in the Republic. Efforts have been made to reduce inefficiences in the social welfare system arising from the poverty/unemployment trap. Above all, a new atmosphere of confidence, a feeling that the Irish economy's problems can be tackled successfully, is gaining ground.

Improvement, not resolution, is the operative word. Unemployment remains at 18 per cent of the labour force, leaving the economy well short of Joe Durkan's definition of competitiveness as a situation where resources are fully employed. The debt/GNP ratio remains extraordinarily high, despite recent fiscal improvements. Also, taxation levels are far too high for an economy seeking to be competitive with the UK and continental Europe. Irish income tax rates of 58 per cent maximum and 35 per cent standard contrast with 40 per cent and 25 per cent in the UK after the 1988 budget. Too many of our talented young people are leaving the country in search of higher rewards, and attracting them back has become a really expensive proposition for Irish business. Much, then, needs to be done.

Without detracting from the recent successes, it is no harm to remember that some of the improvement in the economy's position has been due to favourable external circumstances. By their nature, these factors are, to a greater or lesser degree, capable of being reversed:

— the British economy has been growing steadily, in contrast with its poor performance in the early 1980s, with consequent gains for Irish exports and easing of domestic labour market pressures;
— Ireland's terms of trade have improved significantly, rising by 5 per cent between 1985 and the first quarter of 1988; low oil prices and the weakening dollar played a part in this, as has the rise in export prices of some CAP goods;
— world and domestic interest rates have fallen in nominal terms. For a country with a combined foreign and domestic debt of £26,000 million, every one percentage point fall in interest rates eventually leads to a saving of £260 million. The high interest rates of the first half of the 1980s wreaked havoc with the Coalition Government's budget arithmetic. The deteriorating fiscal position in turn prevented any possibility of domestic Irish interest rates being manoeuvred below the UK level (such as happened in 1988). Between 1987 and 1988, by contrast, interest payments on Irish public debt remained virtually static, notwithstanding the continuous rise in the overall level of debt, because of lower interest rates;
— exchange rate movements involving a weak dollar and a comparatively strong sterling have been favourable to the Irish economy.

Besides these factors, account must also be taken, in analysing the balance of payments turn-around, of the depressed state of domestic demand. Overall demand for investment goods and for consumer durables such as motor cars, both highly import-intensive categories of demand, has been unusually subdued in recent years. A sustained recovery in the economy could easily put the balance of payments under pressure. In the case of motor cars, the decline in new private car registrations from 105,000 in 1981 to 54,000 in 1987 has led to import bill savings of up to £200 million per year at current prices.

STRATEGY FOR COMPETITIVENESS

All this suggests that a strategy for continued growth must give priority to (*a*) fiscal balance, (*b*) lower taxation, (*c*) efficient cost structures, and (*d*) non-price competitive factors.

Fiscal Policy: *There must be no let-up in the progress towards fiscal recovery.* As already noted, Ireland's present debt ratio is inordinately high. As long as it persists at this level, the economy is vulnerable to external interest rate shocks, which could destroy even the best recovery strategy. Moreover, the high burden of debt servicing reduces the Government's capacity to undertake development-oriented initiatives in taxation and reallocation of expenditure.

It is true that, on current estimates, the debt/GNP ratio is near stabilising in 1988. However, the rate of interest on debt—about 8 per cent—continues to exceed the nominal growth of GNP, which means that there will be underlying pressure towards an increase in the debt ratio unless the primary balance (i.e. the difference between Government revenue and expenditure *less* interest payments) remains strongly in surplus. The OECD were surely right to emphasise that, in the fiscal area, further major measures need to be taken in the years beyond 1988, and that *reduction* in the debt ratio must be the target once stabilisation has been achieved. 'Reducing the debt/GNP ratio will require a period of adjustment lasting several years. *Maintaining the momentum of fiscal correction would make Ireland's medium-term prospects brighter than for many years.*' (Emphasis added.)[3]

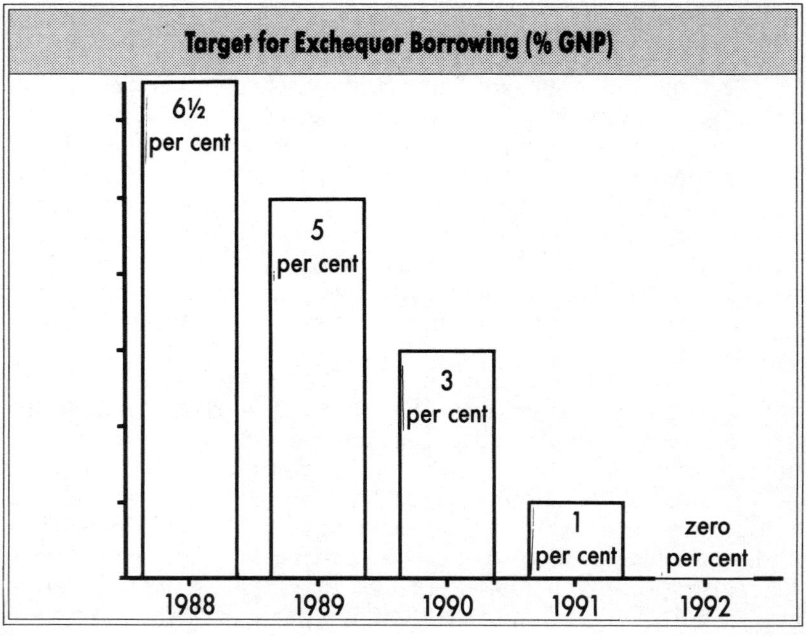

The main source of fiscal correction must be cuts in expenditure. This means focusing on public sector pay, charges for services, economies in health and education, and cuts in the real value of some social welfare transfers and better targeting in others.

A reasonable strategy for the Irish economy would be the complete elimination of the exchequer borrowing rate by 1992 to the schedule shown in the table opposite.

That should leave a sufficient surplus on the non-interest EBR to compensate for any excess of interest rates over GNP growth rates, and it would permit a gradual reduction in the debt/GNP ratio.

Taxation: A small peripheral factor-mobile country such as Ireland cannot afford to have tax rates permanently higher than those of its trading partners. This has been the lesson of bitter experience in the 1980s. In terms of indirect taxation, there is need for a gradual alignment with UK rates and, in the context of completion of the market in 1992, with harmonised EEC rates. Personal taxation must also be reduced. It is not necessary to debate whether high or low rates of taxation are socially desirable or not: the crucial factor is that the economically viable tax level in Ireland is determined by external forces. We are 'tax rate takers', in much the same way as 'price takers', in an internationally competitive environment. The objective of lowering personal income tax therefore would be (1) to encourage talented people to stay in Ireland; (2) to make it easier to attract talented people *back* to Ireland; (3) apart from and in addition to the above, to improve the incentive structure for employers and employees, i.e. to make enterprise rewarding; and (4) to help people escape the unemployment/poverty trap. A practicable target would be to align Irish tax rates to UK and EC levels by 1992, an objective that has the dual merit of conforming to the requirements of completion of the market and of being in Ireland's self-interest economically.

Efficient Cost Structure: Ireland cannot expect to be cost-competitive under every cost heading: distance from markets, for example, imposes an unavoidable cost burden. Hence the objective should be to ensure that the cost structure should be efficient, i.e. should reflect underlying comparative advantage. Given the nation's comparative abundance of well-educated labour, labour costs should be such as to encourage the employment of such people. Because of labour market inflexibilities, this objective has not been achieved. The tax, legal and administrative systems still make hiring labour relatively unattractive. Employer liability insurance costs, for example, are estimated by the Confederation of Irish Industry to be three times the European average, reflecting (*a*) high legal costs associated with claims, (*b*) an excessive level of compensation awards under the jury system (currently being changed), and (*c*) the increasing frequency of claims. These factors intervene between the undoubted attraction of Irish labour costs (in terms of hourly pay and payroll tax) and the market's perception of labour costs (which has to take account of non-payroll costs and level of labour productivity).

A recurring theme of this volume has been the necessity—as long as high unemployment persists—of keeping the rise in Irish pay cuts *below* that of our major trading partners. The opposite was allowed to happen between 1980 and 1986. Irish pay developments during that period lost contact with exchange rate policy and with trends in competing countries.

The energy cost position facing Irish business is improving, though it has been unsatisfactory in the recent past. Electricity prices to Irish industry were considered to be one of the highest in Europe in the early 1980s.[4] Irish industrialists are subject to high petroleum costs by comparison with most countries in the European Community, and a further increase relative to other competing markets has been evident since 1985. In early 1987 they were 36 per cent above the EC average and 39 per cent above UK levels. Business is suffering a significant cost penalty on this score. Internal Irish transport costs are also uncompetitive compared with corresponding costs abroad, partly because of geographical and demographic factors but partly also because of controllable factors such as insurance and petroleum costs and poor road infrastructure.

Interest rates were until recently a major source of competitive disadvantage. Nothing illustrates so well the close interconnection between macroeconomic stability and the business environment than Irish experience in relation to interest rates. Between the first quarter of 1987 and the second quarter of 1988, prime overdraft rates fell from 14 to 8 per cent and mortgage rates from 12½ to under 9 per cent. A major factor supporting this interest rate decline was the improvement in the country's fiscal position. The Government, as a result, needed to borrow less, and in response to a restoration of confidence, capital inflows started to emerge, both of which kept downward pressure on interest rates. The resultant decline helped business directly through lower finance costs, and indirectly by restraining pay demands. Changes in interest rates can, experience shows, have as dramatic an impact on discretionary employee income as changes in income tax. It goes without saying that any indication of the Government's easing up on the objective of fiscal correction would have a very adverse effect on interest rates.

A programme for action under this heading therefore must include (*a*) a continued search for labour market flexibility in the elimination of the poverty/unemployment trap; (*b*) pay increases related explicitly to those in major trading countries, with the objective of keeping them below those rates until the employment position picks up; (*c*) continued monitoring of non-pay costs, such as transport and insurance costs; and (*d*) downward pressure on interest rates to be exerted by means of strong fiscal policy.

Non-Price Factors: Several contributors to this volume have explained the importance of such intangibles as motivation, marketing and product quality in determining competitiveness. Ivor Kenny's *In Good Company* contains an assessment by Denis Brosnan of the Kerry Group of the reasons for the company's success: 'We had absolute commitment to lowest cost production. If you are the lowest cost producer that is the first step on the road to profitability . . . *lowest cost production and get your marketing right.*' (Emphasis added.)[5]

Setting the agenda for these non-price factors would imply continued emphasis on high-quality business and economics training (which does not have to be equated with narrowness or philistinism), emphasis on Continental languages, and engendering a more positive approach to business. The European Management Forum *World Competitiveness Report, 1984,* for example, ranked Ireland among 22 major industrial countries as follows: design, 21; quality, 18; marketing, 22; delivery, 18—hardly an impressive rating!

The idea, indeed, could be broadened, as Leonard Wrigley has done in another context: 'Competitiveness in such factors as product design, quality, marketing and delivery depend very much on industrial relations—on people in business enterprises working well together—as is documented by research on the factors underlying Japan's export success.'[6] Industrial relations, Wrigley goes on to argue, have been dominated by trade union attitudes borrowed lock, stock and barrel from the UK that were completely inappropriate to Irish circumstances.

Attitudes are changing for the better, but bad habits die hard. An instance in 1988 was the closure of the O'Hanlon plant, involving the loss of some two hundred jobs, because of a dispute over a no-strike deal. The principle on which the workers voted themselves out of a job was mystifying to the thousands of employees who had never exercised the strike option in their lives, and must have appeared even more mystifying to the 200,000 unemployed. An editorial in *The Irish Times* on 9 June 1988, following the closure, concluded that no effort should be spared by the Minister for Industry and Commerce to find a replacement industry for Longford. Some people still seem to find nothing odd with blaming all the nation's unemployment on the Government! Attitudes such as these are, it is to be hoped, the dying vestiges of a phase in Irish economic history that caused much unnecessary hardship.

CONCLUSION

It used to be said that future generations would suffer from this generation's careless accumulation of debt. We now know better. The time lag, in the world of economics, between mistakes and consequences is comparatively short—as the thousands on the unemployment register, lists of bankrupt companies and overtaxed employers and employees can all too readily testify. But if retribution comes swiftly in a small open economy such as Ireland, there is a consoling corollary. The rewards of sensible economic policies will not only be reaped by future generations but also by this present one, and it might not have very long to wait. This constitutes a compelling case for continuing the policies of adjustment outlined in the Programme for National Recovery, which have served the country so well.

Notes

1. Department of Finance, *Economic Review and Outlook, 1988,* Dublin: Stationery Office (Pl. 5823) 1988.
2. Seán Barrett, 'Air-Fare Deregulation', Dublin (duplicated) 1988.
3. Organisation for Economic Co-operation and Development, *Economic Survey of Ireland, 1987/88,* Paris: OECD 1987, 80.
4. *Proposal for Plan, 1984–87,* Dublin: Stationery Office 1984, 162.
5. Ivor Kenny (ed.), *In Good Company,* Dublin: Gill and Macmillan 1987, 69.
6. Joseph Lee (ed.), *Ireland: Towards a Sense of Place,* Cork: Cork University Press 1985, 70.